Praise for
The Young Atheist's Handbook

'A touching personal account that makes for a courageous and compelling read. This is among the most powerful and convincing arguments against religion that I have come across, and it is written in a way that is never patronising or trivialising.'
Professor Jim Al-Khalili OBE, physicist and broadcaster

'A book that destroys the cliché of the atheist as joyless rationalist and shows the humanity, love, and concern that often lies behind godless thinking.'
Robin Ince, writer and comedian

'More than just a great handbook, this is an honest and often very moving story about valuing truth over hope, even in the face of grief.'
Tim Minchin, comedian and writer

'Like many bright and curious children before and since, kind teachers, books and school provided the young Alom Shaha with a ladder out of inner-city poverty and an escape from his abusive, feckless father. But *The Young Atheist's Handbook* is no anti-Muslim misery memoir. Rather its strength is the way he explores his life and faith scientifically, through a series of thought experiments. From its taboo-busting opening, when, in a simple experiment, he eats pork for the first time, Alom Shaha's rational exploration of the corrosive power of religious indoctrination is refreshingly down to earth, heartfelt and deeply moving. It combines a raw personal story of his Bangladeshi Muslim background with the understated and carefully researched honesty of a scientist seeking the truth, and of a teacher wanting to free young minds. An inspiring and brave book that speaks for thousands who dare not admit their atheism.'
Samira Ahmed, journalist and broadcaster

'Alom Shaha's *The Young Atheist's Handbook* is moving, heartwarming, and thoughtful ... Many today are despairing, grappling with doubt, or fearful for their lives for wanting to leave Islam and religion. Apostasy is still punishable by death in a number of countries worldwide. Alom's honest journey of why and how he has freed himself from religion's hold will be essential reading for many of them, and it will surely empower and inspire.'
Maryam Namazie, human rights activist

'Alom Shaha has shrugged off the shackles of poverty, racism, and, most of all, religious superstition, to begin to fulfil his potential as a human being. In this wise, compassionate, honest, and often heartbreaking book, he tells of his remarkable journey from a tough inner-city council estate to the rejection of the Islamic beliefs of his Bangladeshi immigrant community. It took a lot of guts to "come out" as a nonbeliever, but Shaha did it to show others who harbour severe doubts about their faith that they are not alone. This is an important and courageous book that needed to be written.'

Marcus Chown, author and broadcaster

'Alom's circumstances will be shared by many young people from Muslim backgrounds growing up today. His personal account of his own experiences will be an indispensable source of comfort for them, and a movingly written insight for any reader.'

Andrew Copson, Chief Executive of the British Humanist Association

'Insightful, conversational, intelligent, enlightening, intimate, and just plain eye-opening. Shaha opens his life, his heart, and his mind to us in a compelling journey towards unbelief.'

Dr Leslie Cannold, author of *The Book of Rachael*

'This is all very annoying. While most of us struggle to put two coherent sentences together, Alom Shaha seems to have knocked out this beautifully written and important book at the same time as teaching physics, and making films. Atheists and religious people alike should read this to see that the path to enlightenment is not always easy, especially if you come from a culture in which being faithless is derided. But more importantly, young people who are working out their own path should read it to see that you can be free to think for yourself.'

Dr Adam Rutherford, science writer and broadcaster

THE
YOUNG
ATHEIST'S
HANDBOOK

THE
YOUNG
ATHEIST'S
HANDBOOK

LESSONS FOR LIVING A GOOD
LIFE WITHOUT GOD

ALOM SHAHA

Biteback Publishing

This edition published in Great Britain in 2012 by
Biteback Publishing Ltd
Westminster Tower
3 Albert Embankment
London SE1 7SP

First published in 2011 by
Scribe Publications Pty Ltd
18–20 Edward St, Brunswick, Victoria, Australia 3056

ISBN 978-1-84954-311-8

10 9 8 7 6 5 4 3 2 1

A CIP catalogue record for this book is available from the British Library.

Printed and bound in Great Britain by
CPI Group (UK) Ltd, Croydon CR0 4YY

For Aslom, Morium, Shahajahan, Shalim, and Lizzie.
Thank you for giving me so much to believe in, and for believing in me.

CONTENTS

I mean, what
What if no one's watching
What if when we're dead
We are just dead
I mean, what
What if it's just us down here
What if God is just an idea
Someone put in your head

ANI DIFRANCO

FOREWORD

ONE OF THE hardest things for any human being to do is to break free from an all-encompassing belief system, and to deal with the response of the community he or she thereby leaves behind. Alom Shaha has done this, with courage and clarity of mind; and in these pages, he tells how he did it. It is a moving story, and a painful one at times, but it is also an optimistic one because it shows how people can free themselves from tradition, superstition, and powerful pressures to conform, even against formidable odds. Alom Shaha's story is about how an individual achieved this, and thereby gained the greatest kind of liberty there is: liberty of mind.

Of course, some will say that Alom had certain advantages: he had a scholarship to a fine school, went on to university, became a physics teacher (a good one, too: I've seen him with his pupils). But note that these things were made possible by his intellect, and the use to which he put it. He learned, and he thought; and early in life he began to think for himself about what his Muslim community in the Elephant and Castle area of London expected him to think. Family and community circumstances, and the circumstances of life in

that part of London during his early years, raised high barriers
to the independent exercise of mind, but he achieved that independence, and here is the result: a book that tells other people
that they can think for themselves and question orthodoxies,
thus freeing themselves from tradition and expectation, and
gaining the same liberty of mind that Alom found.

Unbeknown to Alom, he and I were neighbours during his
childhood. For many years I lived in Trinity Church Square
near the Elephant and Castle, very close to the little Harper
Road library — now, alas, gone — where his early reading
helped him on the road to freedom. I too had a ticket for that
library; perhaps we were frequently in there at the same time.
At election times, I undertook political canvassing for the
Labour Party through the neighbouring estates, in one of
which he lived. For a while, one of my daughters went to the
primary school next to the Harper Road library. I think about
the coincidences in the overlapping lives of people whose
paths must often have crossed, thinking about the same
things, questioning, looking for a true and meaningful forward path in life that was not overshadowed by the crushing
bulk of outdated thought systems. Without any doubt there
are other Aloms in those Elephant and Castle estates, and
likewise in other parts of London, in other parts of the United
Kingdom, and in other parts of the world; other Aloms thinking and doubting and seeking liberation of mind. His book
will be an inspiration to them, and a guide.

His book will be a guide because in telling the story of his
own journey, Alom gives the reasons why he is confirmed in

his atheism, the reasons that reflection, science, and philosophy offered him, and offer anyone with a clear and open mind. It frequently happens that people revise their attitude to the belief system which, when they were children, the adults in their lives obliged them to accept, though not for reasons that they could then articulate in logical order, but instead because they felt that there was something wrong and hollow about that belief system, something which did not ring true. And then, as they proceed to read, discuss, learn, and think, they begin to see the underlying reasons for their intuition, and to build the arguments that confirm their suspicions. This happened to Alom, too. What is admirable about his book is how it presents the logic and evidence along with the story of his development, so that the reader sees how, in Alom's retrospect, the intellectual case for his atheism presented itself to him. He organises that case very cogently and clearly, and I am confident that his account will help many others to a shorter and less painful journey than the one that he had to make. And that, of course, is precisely why he wrote this book.

I warmly recommend the pages that follow, and applaud Alom Shaha for the courage and frankness he displays in them. His book is another lantern on a road that too many people find dark and steep; it illuminates the route to a better destination for all those who seek what Alom found: namely, that precious liberty of mind which makes its possessor open to all good things.

A.C. Grayling
London, 2012

INTRODUCTION

BRINGING HOME THE BACON

I REMEMBER THE first time that I ate bacon. It was a momentous, pivotal moment in my life, requiring courage, strength, and determination. Well, kind of.

It was the summer after my A-levels, and it should have been the best three months of my life so far. I'd spent the last two years studying physics, chemistry, mathematics, and further mathematics, and could finally take a break from the peculiar pressures of that particular combination of subjects. Studying so much maths had frazzled my brain — I would dream of it, waking up convinced that I had proven complex mathematical theorems, glimpsed numerical truths that no one had seen before. Sadly, unlike Srinivasa Ramanujan, an Indian office clerk whose visions astonished the best mathematicians in the world and led him to a place at Cambridge, I could never remember my dreams, and simply woke up frustrated, angry that my maths lessons seemed to have taken over my life. The end of my A-levels marked a milestone — I was to leave the school that I had loved for the past seven years and begin the rest of my life. Yet, before I could do that, I had to spend three months working as a waiter in a fancy London hotel so that I could save up enough money to live on when I left home for university.

I'd like to report that it was an amazing summer, that I went out after every shift to get drunk with my fellow waiters and fell in love with a beautiful waitress, slightly older than me, losing my virginity to her in one of the hotel rooms. That would have been a good story, teen fiction that Judy Blume would be proud to have written, filled with the kind of drama and excitement that I longed for. Sadly, far from being fun, the summer of 1992 was a miserable time for me — unrequited love for a schoolfriend had left my heart broken, and I was wracked with guilt at the thought of leaving my brothers and sister in an unhappy home while I went off to university. And there was no time to enjoy being finished with school: now that my academic work was over, I took on as many £4-an-hour shifts as the hotel had available, often working 18 hours a day.

Yet although I didn't lose my virginity at the hotel, it was there, in a quiet moment away from the demands of rich, aging Americans and Japanese tour groups, that I would do something for the first time that was, at least to me, almost as significant.

The breakfast shift was hell — I'd have to get up at 5.00 a.m. to make my way to work for a 6.15 start. As it was summertime, the hotel was full, and the restaurant was packed from the minute the doors opened until the breakfast service ended four hours later. Even though the customers served themselves from a buffet, the work was non-stop. It was not unusual to spend the entire shift on my feet, ferrying cups of tea and coffee, clearing away endless crockery, and wiping down and re-laying tables. I can't eat first thing in the morning and usually start my day with nothing but a mug of tea, so that's all I'd be functioning on through the morning. Even those waiters who'd been smart enough to have breakfast would be starving by the end of the shift. If we were lucky — that is, if the right manager was on duty — we could help ourselves to the leftovers from the buffet at the end of service.

It was on one such morning when one of my colleagues, a Chinese guy about the same age as me, held up a rasher of bacon and said, 'This is delicious … I dare you to try it.' He knew that I was Bangladeshi and so, as people still do today, assumed that I was Muslim — an assumption that wasn't entirely incorrect, as I had indeed been brought up under Islam. He knew he was being deliberately provocative by holding a piece of pork so close to my face, but he wasn't being malicious; it was just part of the banter and messing around that made the job a little less depressing. I don't think he expected me to do what I did in response: reach over, take the bacon, put it in my mouth, and eat it, before declaring, 'You're right, it is delicious.' The look on his face was as delectable as the bacon. It was a spontaneous decision, but I suspect that I would have eaten bacon at some time or another while working that job — I smelled it every day, and had been tempted to try it.

I wanted to try bacon not just because it smelled good, but also because I wanted to commit this act of rebellion against the religion I had been brought up to believe in but had largely rejected. I wanted to prove to myself that I didn't really think I would be struck down by lightning if I did it; that I didn't believe I would be punished, either in this life or the next; and that there was nothing intrinsically 'wrong' with eating pork, and my fear of doing so was irrational. I immediately liked the taste of bacon — it had a wonderful flavour, extremely savoury and unlike any other meat I had tasted. The only negative thing was the visible disgust on the face of one of the other waiters, a friend of mine and fellow Bangladeshi, who took his religion a little more seriously.

I suspect that this event made little impression on my colleagues, and that they will have long forgotten it. But for me, it was a turning point. Not only had I eaten bacon, but I had done so in front of one of my Muslim friends. This seemingly insignificant act was incredibly liberating, allowing me to leave behind years of an unsettling discomfort in thinking of myself as Muslim. That morning, I underwent my own small but significant rite of passage — and I have never had a full English breakfast without bacon since.

Today, I am a regular consumer of bacon and a host of other porcine products, from the fabulously crispy pork in cheap Chinese restaurants to my brother's delicious chilli-and-chorizo pasta sauce. This admission may be the most controversial thing I write in this book, the confession that turns many readers away in disgust. Because, to millions of people around the world, the very thought of eating pork is anathema.

I was one of a number of Bangladeshi children who arrived in the United Kingdom during the 1970s as part of a wave of immigration. Most of us had come from villages with no plumbing or electricity, and there were a lot of new things to get used to. One of my clearest memories from my earliest days in England is of my mother finding me squatting on top of a toilet instead of sitting on it. I was unaware of just how marvellous the toilet was: not only did it flush waste away, but it was designed to sit on while doing your business.

I quickly grew accustomed to my new world, and close to the top of the list of new things I loved were the free meals that all of us immigrants were entitled to at our South London primary school. Before this, we had not eaten anything except traditional Bangladeshi food — mostly rice and curry. Chicken pies, roast beef, and baked beans were as exotic to us as samosas and onion bhajis were to English children back then. (It was long before political correctness or Jamie Oliver would have any influence on school lunch menus.) Some Bangladeshi children struggled to appreciate the strange and unusual flavours of British cuisine; but for many of us, the food tasted wondrous, and we lapped it all up. We were delighted when offered seconds and, on particularly lucky days, thirds. We would happily eat even the grey, overboiled cabbage that was mostly rejected by the English-born children; soaked in lashings of gravy, it was a savoury treat unlike anything we were fed at home.

With the exception of a few hardcore Muslims, our parents were okay with us eating chicken, lamb, or beef, and turned a blind eye to the fact that the meat was not halal. Being poor, they were just glad that we were getting free meals. However, this bending of the Islamic rules did not extend to pork, and the teachers were 'culturally aware' enough to tell us that we couldn't have it. So we Bangladeshi children would always have the 'second choice' meal whenever there were sausages, and it was never as tasty as I imagined the sausages to be.

School lunches played a part, albeit a small one, in my eventual rejection of the religion I was brought up with. There seemed to be no evidence that pork was bad for you: the non-Muslim children ate their sausages with impunity, and it grated on me that they didn't seem to have any rules or regulations constraining what they could or could not eat.

There were other things at primary school which made me suspect that I had gotten a raw deal in having been born Muslim. The non-Muslim kids (most of whom were Christian) didn't have to go to church after school, as we had to go to mosque every day; they didn't seem to spend much time worrying about being 'good Christians' in the way that we were always being told to be 'good Muslims'; and their lives in general did not seem to revolve around religion in the way that ours were supposed to. I would never have admitted it, but as a child I was convinced that Christians had a better religion. Their bible seemed to be full of nice stories about this lovely man called Jesus — which is how Christianity was presented to us in school and in the *Stories from the Bible*-type books I picked up in the library. I couldn't even read 'our' holy book because it was written in Arabic and, according to our local imam, all it seemed to say was that we should be really, really scared of Allah and that anyone who was not a Muslim was going to burn in the fires of hell for eternity. Christianity seemed to be a gentler, less demanding, more reasonable religion. Clearly, I wasn't in possession of all the relevant facts, but these were the conclusions I had arrived at based on my education thus far.

Of all the things that I envied about my non-Muslim classmates, it was Christmas that really made me wish to be one of them. Christmas was a wonderful, magical day that we would spend weeks building up to at school. We'd make decorations, sing carols, play pass the parcel, and act out the Nativity. Multiculturalism, with its emphasis on celebrating religious diversity, had not yet been introduced to the classroom: there was no sense that making such a big deal out of Christmas might not be an entirely sensitive thing to do when a large proportion of the school's population was not Christian. Not aware that my cultural sensitivities should have been hurt, I loved it. Christmastime at school was brilliant: there'd be a special lunch, and musical chairs, and a general having of the kind of fun that Muslims never seemed to have. The Ayatollah Khomeini once wrote, 'Allah did not create man so that he could have fun', and at times it felt to me like this was the dominant theme of Islam — the forbidding of fun.

Those few weeks before Christmas were the best of the school year. They would fly by all too quickly, and leave me sad in the knowledge that Christmas was over for me but only just beginning for the lucky kids who weren't Muslim. Most other children would leave school knowing that they were about to get amazing presents and have the best time ever (or so I imagined), while we Bangladeshis had to console ourselves with the fact that there would be lots of good stuff on television for a couple of weeks. The closest Muslim celebration, Eid, seemed lame in comparison, despite coming around twice a year instead of just once.

I didn't eat a pork sausage until several years after leaving primary school. It was only once I'd eaten my first piece of bacon, at the age of 18, that I went on to discover the culinary delights of sausages, from the traditional English ones served with breakfast at the hotel to pepperoni, which took my enjoyment of pizza to a new level. My parents' simple instruction not to eat pork doesn't quite explain why it took me so long to contravene the Islamic prohibition against pork, or why so many Muslims stick to it so 'religiously'. From my experience and what I've seen of other apostates, it seems to me that eating pork is the last taboo, the final rule of Islam, that a Muslim will break before facing up to the fact that he or she is indeed a kafir, an infidel. I'm not being entirely facetious; I know people who call themselves Muslims but regularly drink alcohol — something that is more strictly forbidden in the Qur'an than eating pork. I know others who gamble, fornicate, and commit countless other 'sins', but pride themselves on having never touched a pork product, let alone eaten one. This may seem ridiculous, but I think that it is testimony to the power of childhood indoctrination and what an overwhelming emotion disgust can be.

A page titled 'Great Facts on Pork' on *Islam — The Modern Religion* website states that 'eating the meat of the pig is said to contribute to lack of morality and shame, plus greed for wealth, laziness, indulgence, dirtiness and gluttony'.[1] While this exact message may not be expounded in all Muslim homes, Muslim children, and indeed Jewish children, are taught from a very young age that pork is 'unclean' and 'disgusting'. This explains why the idea of eating pork elicits such a deep feeling of revulsion from many Jews and Muslims, and why it is deeply offensive in these cultures to refer to people as 'swine'. The word 'unclean' has powerful connotations, and telling children that something is disgusting is sufficient to make them disgusted by it, even if they have no direct experience of the offending object. Scientists think that disgust evolved to protect us from eating things that might have made us ill, such as decaying corpses or faecal matter. So, at a time when pigs often carried worm larvae and other disease-causing organisms, being disgusted by the thought of eating pork provided a useful protection mechanism. But these things are not an issue today — refrigeration and greater awareness of hygiene in food preparation mean that eating pork is no more dangerous than eating any other meat.

In my experience, Muslims have a stronger aversion to eating pork than Jews do. I've met and come across a number of

Jews who enjoy bacon,[2] but Muslims who openly admit to
eating pork are rare (although I have met one or two who
have been unable to resist the occasional slice of pepperoni
pizza). It might not be an exaggeration to say that some
Muslims would rather die than eat pork, even though my
understanding is that Allah would excuse eating it if there
were no alternative but to starve. The thing is, I understand
and empathise with the aversion that Muslims have to eating
pork, and why so many Muslims who are otherwise lapsed
refuse to touch it, because it took me years to get over my
own reluctance, to overcome the effects of childhood conditioning and take what was probably the final step in admitting
to myself that I was not a Muslim and did not believe in God.

The rest of this book is loosely my story of how and why
I choose to call myself an atheist. I am going to say up-front
that I know that many of the ideas and arguments I present
may be approached in different ways, and that some of the
concepts may be more nuanced than I have presented them.
I am not aiming to critically examine these issues in all their
complexity, or to provide an academic treatise on why religion is wrong, but to give a personal take on how I see people
interacting with religion, based on my experiences.

I am a science teacher, and if I were to be strictly scientific
I ought to call this book *The Young Agnostic's Handbook*. But
my use of the word 'atheist' is a deliberate attempt to use it
as I think it should be used in the modern world — not as a
scientific term, but as an identity label that signifies important
beliefs. I, like millions of others, choose to call myself an

atheist because it tells those around me that I actively reject ideas that the majority of the world's population identify with, ideas that have shaped the major religions and continue to play a significant role in the lives of billions of individuals. It lets people know that I do not believe in the existence of the God of the Abrahamic religions, nor in any other anthropo-morphic god or supernatural being. But calling myself an atheist doesn't just tell people about what I don't believe — it also tells them that I think you can lead a happy, worthwhile, and good life without believing in God.

More people than ever before are choosing to label them-selves as atheists. It is a statement that we think we ought to live in a world that is not governed by rules based on ancient civilisations. We think that humans are responsible for our moral choices, that humans can only look to one another for hope in times of despair, and that humans are the most marvellous thing in the universe.

In this book, I have tried to use my experiences as a teacher and what I recall of my journey towards atheism in a way that I hope will make sense to those who are just starting out on their way to think about these issues. I hope that it will provide an informal guide to rejecting religion, not only for young people, but also for adults who are new to atheism — people who are 'young atheists' in a different sense. I hope that the story I tell might provide comfort and reassurance to those who need it, and that it will confirm it is okay to leave behind the religion of your childhood and find other ways to make sense of the world. My intention in this book is not to tell anyone what to think, but merely to say, 'Here are some ideas that I have encountered, which have made me think about religion. Join me in thinking about this stuff.' This is very much my story, incorporating my beliefs about these things; yours will be different.

ONE

THE DAY GOD DIED

I WAS PLAYING football when my mother died.

She was in an intensive care unit at Guy's — the same London hospital in which all of her children, except me, had been born. Kicking a ball around with my friends, I was as oblivious of her as she was of me. At some point, a doctor would have pulled a plug or pushed a button and declared my mother's life to be finished. At that moment, I would have been filled with life, in the way that only a 13-year-old running around a football pitch can be.

My mother, mum, 'Amma', had been in hospital for months, in and out of a coma at least a couple of times. She'd been pregnant with my youngest brother at an age when, given her medical history, she really shouldn't have been. It probably came as no surprise to the doctors that the pregnancy led to medical complications, the nature of which I never understood beyond the fact that it had something to do with her heart not working properly. When she fell into a coma, my brother was prematurely removed from her womb — it doesn't seem correct to say that he was 'born' when it was so obvious that he was not ready to be separated from his mother. He was so tiny that my father could hold him in the palm of his hand; at least, he could have held him if my brother wasn't wired up to a bunch of machines and perforated with countless plastic tubes.

My mother suffered from all sorts of medical problems, but it was mental illness that landed her in hospital on what seemed to be a regular basis when we were growing up. My father and the other Bangladeshi adults around us openly described my mother as *fagol*, which means 'crazy'; some even said she was possessed. So we children thought of our mum as loony, when in fact she was very, very ill. It was only as an adult that I learned she had suffered from bipolar disorder or, as it used to be known, 'manic depression'; but putting a name to something that caused her so much suffering has not made it easier to accept what a tortured existence she must have had.

The periods when she was depressed don't particularly stand out in my memory, except for a vague recollection of incomprehension as to why my mother was so sad. But the trauma of her psychotic episodes is still fresh in my mind, including one incident in which she dangled my newly born brother over the balcony of our flat. When a psychotic episode took hold of her, her behaviour would become increasingly erratic: she would become sexually disinhibited and, eventually, so violent that she would need to be locked up. She once managed to kick down a hospital door and run all the way home, barefoot, in the middle of the night. (I imagine that hospital security has improved since then.) You can imagine how terrifying it was for us to see our mother in this state, but by far the worst thing about it was that she seemed to completely forget who we were: she didn't recognise the people who loved her most in the world, those whose happiness depended, so very much, on her.

She died before I was mature enough to take an interest in her as a person. I envy all those who get to know their mums and dads as people in their own right — what a privilege, joy, and honour that must be, to be friends with your parents. For many years, I have been consumed with piecing together as much of my mother's life as I am able to, relying on memories of relatives and friends. I treasure even the smallest anecdote about her, from brief encounters recollected by my childhood friends to stories of her adolescence from those who knew her then. The one person who could have told me most about her, my father, was the only one I never asked; he died before either of us was sensible enough to mend our relationship so that, at the very least, we could have had the only conversation we really should have had.

My mother spent the first few years of her marriage in Bangladesh. By all accounts, she was mostly happy. However, it took her years to get pregnant, far longer than anyone had expected. Her first child died soon after he was born, leaving her 'mindless' with grief, according to my aunts and uncles. This may have been the first of the many episodes of severe depression that would plague her for the rest of her life. I was born a couple of years later, slightly premature but healthy nonetheless. My father left for England soon after, aiming to earn enough money so that we could join him, but this was not such a blow to my mother's happiness now that she had her much-longed-for child.

Inevitably, my mother spoiled me. My aunts teased her about it back then. Today, they reminisce fondly about how she was so loath to put me down or have me out of her sight that she would tie me to her sari. Apparently, rather than have anyone else watch over me, she once tied me to a tree while she bathed herself (there were no baths or showers in our village at the time, so we washed in an outdoor *furki*, a large pond teeming with plants and fish). While she was washing, I busied myself with covering my body in as much dirt as I could. My aunts ridiculed her for not beating me: how else would I learn?

For the record, she did attempt to beat me when I was a bit older — I must have been more than a handful for her — but I remember laughing as she chased me around the kitchen with a wooden spoon. She just could not bring herself to hit me hard enough to make her point.

I was not jealous when my brother was born, a few years after me. He was an adorable, beautiful baby that no one could resist picking up. If anything, he was more spoiled by my mother than I was, but she had enough love to go around; I never felt replaced or less loved or any of those other emotions that first children are said to experience upon the birth of a sibling. Other siblings quickly followed, and by the time my mother died there were five of us: four boys and a girl.

As a result of her illness, my siblings and I had a part-time mother. I can't speak for my brothers or sister, but I resented her for this, even if I didn't consciously realise it at the time. I was angry at her for leaving us, as things were always better when she was around. I was angry at her for making me miss her. And how I missed her; how awful it was to carry around that emptiness every day at school, pretending that nothing was wrong and nursing the hope that she'd be home when I got back from school. But I got used to it, and so did my siblings, because kids do get used to things.

Dr Robert Buckman, in his book *Can We Be Good Without God?*, writes that 'our parents are our first gods'. They are the 'caring, benign, powerful' figures who look after our needs when we cannot do this for ourselves.[1] When we are children and in trouble or need of comfort, we do not pray to an invisible, imaginary being; we turn to our parents. My mother's presence in the world was enough to make me feel safe, protected. When she was well, it was evident in everything she did that we were the centre of her universe: it shone through in the way she fed us, bathed us, held us. Even today, relatives comment on how much she adored us. We knew it. And we know it to this day because the knowledge of her love buried itself deep within us, in a place where it has been, and continues to be, an anchor to hold us strong through the troubles of life.

My experiences as a teacher have led me to believe that pretty much all a child needs to grow up okay is at least one parent who really loves them. Being loved can be a source of great strength to a child, but only if he or she knows it. I have met people who have naïvely argued that all parents love their children, but I don't think that is necessarily true. My siblings and I all work with young people — my sister as a paediatrician, and my brothers and I in schools and youth clubs — and each of us can recount heartbreaking stories of the deliberate neglect and abuse of children. We have all seen evidence that love can make up for whatever other deprivations a child may have to deal with, but pretty much nothing can make up for being deprived of love.

I can't help feeling sorry for my younger siblings because they had even less time with our mother than I did. We share the heartbreaking knowledge that our own children will never know someone who would have been the best grandmother to them. In many ways, I have been a parent to my siblings, and a large part of my own happiness and sense of fulfilment in life comes from having seen them grow up, without coming to harm, into decent, kind, accomplished adults. The pride I have in them is tinged with a deep sadness that my mother never got to see how they turned out. But my greatest pity is reserved for my youngest brother, because he never experienced for himself what it was liked to be loved by her.

I can't remember if my father asked me and my siblings if we wanted to go to the hospital with him the day my mother died. I suspect that he didn't see the point in taking us along.

But I knew something was up — that morning, a bunch of relatives had turned up at our house. They clearly knew what my father was about to do. We children were not warned or braced, by our father or anyone else, for what was going to happen. There was certainly no counselling for us, as I expect there would be these days, but I don't blame my father — it would have been outside his experience or education to know that children need preparation for such situations. My father, though cruel in many ways, was not being deliberately cruel on this occasion.

By that point, my mother had been in hospital for so long that we had become used to her not being at home, and used to seeing a comatose figure when we did visit. After the first few times, we didn't cry at her bedside, but just sat there thinking about other things, at a loss for what to do or even what to feel. Soon, going to hospital became a chore, and we were pleased when we were left behind to play. We were not bad children; we were just children.

When my father returned from the hospital that day, a relative shouted down from the flat, telling me to come up. I don't remember where my siblings were or what they were doing. I'm sure it's not just self-centredness that means I only remember myself and my experiences on that day; I have never spoken to any of my siblings about that moment when we first found out that she was dead.

As I ran up the stairs to our flat, I think part of me guessed what had happened. I remember charging through the door and being pulled aside by a relative, a woman in her twenties, a long-distance aunt or cousin of some sort. I didn't know who she was, or perhaps I just don't remember. What I recall is that she pulled me to her and said, in Bangla, 'Your mother is no more.' That's a precise translation of her words: 'Your mother is no more.' I remember emitting some sort of feral yell, crumpling to the floor, and crying so hard that it hurt. The young woman tried to hold me, but she must have known how futile it was to try to comfort me. I just remember sobbing and sobbing and feeling dizzy, as if I was falling out of space and time, leaving reality. And in a way I was, because in that instant my reality was irrevocably changed.

I was inconsolable then, and I am still inconsolable today. Nothing that has happened in my life since that moment, nothing I believe and nothing I know, can provide consolation. This is why I suspect that I am in some way predisposed not to believe in God, because God is the only thing that could have provided any solace. Death gives birth to gods; without death, there would be fewer gods, if any. The finality of death confronted me at the age of 13 and took away the person whom I loved most. When I touched my mother's cold face at her funeral, there was no comfort for me from any make-believe notion that she would be warm and alive again in some magical heaven. If I had felt that there was an afterlife, believe me, I would have killed myself then and there to join her.

The death of a loved one is probably the most emotionally difficult thing that any of us has to deal with. Inventing a god is a coping strategy that has been adopted by people since prehistoric times, and it is understandable: the emotional disturbance that results from the death of someone close is so debilitating that people cannot be blamed for seeking help wherever they can get it. Perhaps the idea that the death of a loved one is part of some plan that God has for all of us, that it is in some way 'God's will', is a consoling one for some people; perhaps the idea that their loved one has gone to 'be with God' somehow lets some people accept the unacceptable. But not for me; not for me. No idea about God, no religious belief, has provided me with any comfort. It never has and, I suspect, it never will.

Only a few people are so convinced of a life after death that they would do anything to hasten their passage there. Yet many, if not most, adults cling to the idea of some form of afterlife, like children who believe that Narnia is around the corner, waiting for them to stumble into it. But while Narnia is described in glorious detail by C.S. Lewis, I suspect that most adults would struggle to describe the precise nature of the afterlife they believe in.

Ancient cultures used to bury their dead with provisions for the afterlife, indicating that they believed it was in some ways a continuation of this life: a person would need food, clothes, and money. People of these cultures imagined their afterlives as somehow better, grander versions of their current lives, and the appeal of that idea is obvious. It is the kind of afterlife that is portrayed in many films and books; indeed, this is how C.S. Lewis portrays it in *The Last Battle*, the final book of *The Chronicles of Narnia*.

Today, some people may believe that the afterlife is a physical place where one exists in a human body, but a more widespread belief is that only the soul survives death and somehow goes on to live forever. This idea of an 'eternal soul' is central to many modern religions. The soul is seen as permanent and valuable, whereas the body is seen as temporary and in some sense extrinsic, able to be discarded. In myths and stories, it is always our soul the devil is interested in, not our bodies.

It is not necessary to believe in God or to be religious to think that the human soul exists. To an extent, this is an idea that resonates with everyone because we are, by our natures, dualists when it comes to this — our brains work in such a way as to create the feeling that 'we' exist as entities beyond our physical selves, and so it is easy for us to believe that our bodies are mere containers for our souls while we are in this material world. In some sense, this is indeed true: even though our thoughts and feelings may only exist because our bodies exist, they are of course not physical objects that can be touched, observed, or studied in the same way that the cells and organs of our bodies can. Science is making tremendous progress in finding out which bits of the brain are active when we think and feel certain things but, as any good scientist would be quick to point out, that's not the same as knowing what a thought or a feeling is.

There are no special components that make up a human; we are made of the same protons, neutrons, and electrons as every other living thing. It is remarkable that billions of atoms can come together and make a person, but it is somehow jarring or unacceptable to most of us to believe that this is all we are. The evidence suggests that what we think of as our soul is very much the result of physical processes — electrical pulses and chemical reactions — in our brain. Francis Crick, most famous for his work with James Watson in discovering the structure of DNA, puts it like this: 'You, your joys and your sorrows, your memories and your ambitions, your sense of personal identity and free will, are in fact no more than the behaviour of a vast assembly of nerve cells and their associated molecules.'[2]

This was brought home to me in a dramatic, tragic, and incontrovertible way one morning in 2001. My youngest brother, Shalim, is one of those people who can truly be described as inspirational. His premature birth resulted in complications that left him with physical disabilities and learning difficulties. As a toddler, both his legs were broken, suspiciously, while the rest of us were at school, and he spent months in hospital while they healed. He was in and out of hospital throughout his childhood, undergoing numerous painful operations as doctors tried to fix problems with his leg muscles caused by cerebral palsy. Some time later, a cup of boiling tea was spilled on him, leaving him severely scalded and requiring yet another trip to hospital. Yet despite the endless reasons he had to be miserable, Shalim was constantly cheerful and affectionate, a joy to be around. Of course, my siblings and I worried about his future, but he flourished at the special school he attended, and it soon became evident that he would be far more capable of taking care of himself than we had dared to hope.

But our happiness at his success was to be short-lived. On the morning of 21 February 2001, just after he had turned 16, my brother woke up, locked himself in the bathroom, and refused to come out. When we broke through the door, it was immediately apparent that something was very, very wrong. Shalim had smeared shampoo and shower gel all over the walls and was convinced that we, the people who were committed to taking care of him, were going to harm him. We managed to restrain him and take him to hospital, where we were told that he was having a psychotic break-down.

Shalim spent the best part of the next six months in the most wretched place I have ever been, a place where the absence of God is in stark evidence — a children's mental-health ward. More than one of the patients had been admitted after attempting suicide. Of all the sad children I saw there, though, the saddest was a boy who told us that he wished he was Shalim, because 'you come to visit him'. Shalim's misfortunes were mitigated by the love and care we showed for him — things that came naturally to us, but clearly not to the families of many children in that place.

Initially, my siblings and I visited Shalim every day. When it became evident that he was going to be in hospital indefinitely, we went in pairs, alternating the days on which we came. In the whole six months that he was there, my father only visited a handful of times.

For what seemed like ages, Shalim seemed not to recognise us, and often treated our visits with indifference. His love of comic books manifested itself in a cruel way: Shalim seemed to think that he was a superhero and, sometimes, he would confront us with a fighting stance as we entered his room, perhaps imagining that we were the villains he had sworn to defeat. We found this tragically comic at the time, but were more disturbed by the fact that, like my mother had done when she was ill, Shalim had also become sexually disinhibited. This element of his behaviour was particularly unsettling for us, as well as awkward for those around him to deal with.

For the first few months, Shalim was nothing like the young, vivacious boy we knew and loved. He had the same body (although he rapidly lost weight), but he was not the same person, and it was easy to see how this sort of illness could be explained by the idea of someone being possessed by another spirit. Of course, Shalim was not possessed; like my mother before him, Shalim was very, very ill. Something had gone wrong with his brain, and it was only by feeding him the right dosages of mood-stabilising and anti-psychotic drugs that the doctors were eventually able to restore him to his 'normal' self. In many ways, he was 'resurrected' by the chemicals in those drugs because, without them, the Shalim we knew and loved simply didn't exist. The scientific, evidence-based treatment used by the doctors was crucial to his recovery, in a way that no exorcism or any amount of praying could ever have been. My brother's breakdown was, for me, striking evidence that there is no mind–brain duality, that there is no soul, and that a 'person' is very much a result of electrical and chemical happenings in the brain.

Seeing Shalim like this brought back horrible memories of my mother's illness. When his breakdown first occurred, I was terrified that something similar could happen to me or another of my siblings. The doctors told us that this was unlikely — we were all old enough that it would have happened already if it was going to. But this doesn't mean I'm safe from losing myself in the way that Shalim did: I could still develop Alzheimer's, or hit my head and injure my brain, both of which would result in damage that would change my personality, perhaps to the point where I would not really be 'myself' anymore. There are volumes filled with case studies of people who, through some sort of illness or misfortune, have had their neurological function damaged in such a way that their personality has been altered beyond recognition — a fact that genuinely scares me.

All the evidence is that our souls, our minds, our 'selves', are inseparable from our brains. Humans have long known that ingesting certain chemicals can alter the way we think and feel. In the past, people may have thought that eating, drinking, or even smoking certain things gave them access to a spiritual realm, but scientists today believe that such activities lead to chemical changes in the brain that manifest as mental experiences. As well as analysing chemical changes, scientists can now use equipment to administer electrical voltages or magnetic fields directly to our brains, showing a cause-and-effect relationship between physical events in our brains and how we feel or think. These advances in science leave very little doubt that a large part of who we are is determined by physical phenomena that occur inside our heads; while they may not know precisely what it is that happens in our brains to give us the sensation of having a soul, scientists are confident that *something* happens in our brains to make us think or feel anything.

Trying to understand how the brain works is one of the most exciting areas of scientific research. New instruments such as fMRI scanners may open up the brain for us in the way that microscopes allowed us to see the world of cells and particle accelerators allowed us to probe the fundamental building blocks of matter. But perhaps we will never know exactly how the brain works, how that lump of meat inside our skulls gives rise to the marvellous, beautiful thing that it is to be human. Perhaps we will never truly understand what it is that makes us sentient, capable of writing poetry, making music, doing science; perhaps we will never know what it is that allows us to truly live while other animals merely exist.

In a poem he read out to the National Academy of Sciences in 1955, the great physicist Richard Feynman described humans as 'atoms with consciousness, matter with curiosity'.[3] But we are more than the atoms of which we are made, more than the sum of our parts. We are the experiences we have and the memories, knowledge, and beliefs we hold. We really do transcend the physical origins of our being, and I don't mean this in a New Age, spiritual sense. As the writer Kenan Malik put it in his essay 'In Defence of Human Agency':

> To talk of humans as 'transcendent' is not to ascribe to them spiritual properties. It is, rather, to recognise that as subjects we have the ability to transform our selves, our natures, our world, an ability denied to any other physical being. In the six million years since the human and chimpanzee lines first diverged on either side of Africa's Great Rift Valley, the behaviour and lifestyles of chimpanzees have barely changed. Human behaviour and lifestyles clearly have. Humans have learnt to learn from previous generations, to improve upon their work, and to establish a momentum to human life and culture that has taken us from cave art to quantum physics and the conquest of space. It is this capacity for constant innovation that distinguishes humans from all other animals. All animals have an evolutionary past. Only humans make history.[4]

The thought of being temporary is one that the human mind wants to reject, and there may well be good evolutionary reasons for this. But all of the evidence points to the fact that our minds can only exist for as long as our brains do. A scientific understanding of the world makes it hard to believe in an eternal soul. If you want some consolation, there are some scientists who believe that we may one day be able to 'download' ourselves into another type of brain, a more resilient, longer lasting memory- and thought-storage device that will allow us to 'live' for much longer, perhaps for as long as the universe exists. But this is wild speculation, and little comfort for those of us who fear death. It is certainly not as comforting a notion as the idea of eternal life that most religions offer.

Despite there not being a shred of evidence for it, the idea of life after death is a key feature of all the major religions. I've really got to hand it to the Christians, in particular — they've come up with a story in which the hero literally rises from the dead and floats up into the sky. If you can believe that this actually happened — and apparently millions of people do — you can believe that death is not the end, that it is conquerable. Sadly, even though I knew of this story as a child, and even though I was aware that Muslims also had a heaven, I never bought into the idea. I suspect this is not only because it all seemed too good to be true, but also because the evidence that my mother was gone was too hard to ignore.

It's an insidious idea, this notion that there is life after death. The promise of a reward in the afterlife has been used as an excuse to deny help to the poor, helpless, and oppressed; to explain away human misery rather than deal with it. It is an idea that is used to encourage young men and women to kill themselves, and others, so that they can become martyrs. It allows victims of injustice to be told not to worry because justice will be done in the afterlife. It depresses me to think that so many people on the planet live their lives with this notion. Can we truly fulfil our potential as a species as long as we hold on to, and encourage, the perpetuation of the lie of life after death?

People seem to struggle with the notion that this life is all there is. Many seem to think that if they accept that this is it, life has no meaning. A friend once compared this to saying that a cake has no meaning once you've eaten it. A cake provides you with a pleasurable experience, a focus for celebration, a memory, and even perhaps a wish. An eaten cake will give you energy. Some of its atoms may literally become part of you through the processes that are continually replacing the billions of cells in your body. Similarly, when you die, your memory and the things you did will live on for a while, but your atoms will live on for a lot longer, becoming part of other objects in the universe. Ultimately, though, 'you' cease to exist once your atoms stop doing all those things they need to be doing in order to make you alive.

As a child, I used to be scared of this idea. I would sometimes find myself lying in bed, imagining what it would be like not to exist. I used to picture myself buried underground, and would feel a sense of suffocation at the thought of not being 'here' anymore. The concept of nothingness was incredibly frightening to me. But, like most children, I simply grew out of this fear.

When my mother died, I knew that I would never see her again, never get to speak to her, never hold her or be held by her. I've come to accept that. But every so often, I dream about her. Sometimes I spend entire afternoons with her: we go out for meals, we talk endlessly, we just hang out. Sometimes, despite being a grown man, I am sitting in her lap, being held like a child. It's only ever just the two of us; we might pass strangers on the streets as we go for a walk, but no one else is involved in these meetings. These dreams feel so real, I start crying when I wake up and realise that they are not. If I were a believer, I might be able to console myself with the notion that my mother is somehow speaking to me from beyond the grave. But I cannot ignore all the evidence to the contrary, and am forced to accept that these dreams are a result of wishful thinking, of my brain doing incredible things to create a virtual reality of infinite verisimilitude. Despite this, I am grateful for these dreams, and live in the hope of having another.

I visited my mother's grave a number of times in the first few years after she died, mostly out of a sense of duty. I stopped going in my late teens. My siblings and I went to see it a few years ago, soon after my father died. We cried beside it, but felt nothing towards the grave itself — it was just a plot of ground. Today, it is no doubt covered with weeds. For years, the only marker was a cheap wooden board because my father didn't buy a proper gravestone for it — a final insult to a wife whom he had treated poorly throughout her life. I hated him for this, and swore I would buy a gravestone when I could afford it. But I never bought that stone; instead, years later, I had the Bangla word for mother, 'amma', tattooed on my arm. I enjoyed the pain, and it felt like it meant more to permanently scar myself with a reminder of her than to buy a stone. In many respects, it's silly, I know. But then again, you might say that of all the other ways we choose to deal with this unbearable, unavoidable thing we call death.

The death of a parent is a defining moment in the lives of most people, particularly when it occurs in childhood. For me, because of the kind of man my father was, it was the moment when I became an adult, someone for whom no one else was ultimately responsible. It was also the moment when things went from bad to worse for my siblings and me, the point from which we were to become outsiders among the community we had grown up in, and after which we would largely be left to fend for ourselves. It was also perhaps the moment when I first explicitly rejected God.

There is a line in the movie *The Crow* when the hero chastises a drug addict who is neglecting her child by saying, 'Mother is the name for God on the lips and hearts of all children.'[5] I cried when I heard that line because when my mum died, God died, too.

TWO

BEING GOOD

My FATHER USED to beat us when we were children if we did anything he considered bad. The beatings ranged in severity from a slap across the face with his hand to smacks all over our bodies with one of his slippers, the soles of which were made of an improbably hard plastic that had no give when smashed against flesh. Yet, of the many things we resented him for when we were children, this was not one of them.

Like pretty much all of the Bangladeshi children we grew up with, and indeed many of the other children we knew, we accepted that it was our parents' right to beat us if we misbehaved. It was back when corporal punishment was still legal in British schools, so we could expect to be beaten by our teachers, too. Being beaten for bad behaviour was just a fact of life, and we had no notion that our parents and teachers might have been more in the wrong for beating us than we were for whatever we had done to merit it.

My friends and siblings look back on those times and joke

about the beatings we were given. We compare the implements used by our parents, from wooden spoons to various types of sticks — and, of course, the favourite of fathers around the world, the belt. Despite being able to joke about it now, we're all more than aware that, at least sometimes, our parents' punishments bordered on horrific abuse, and we all have a story of our worst beating. For me, it was the time I got caught stealing in the local shopping centre.

Like many children, I went through a phase of shoplifting. It wasn't something I did because I was poor (even though we were indeed poor) or particularly wanted the things I was stealing. It was because shoplifting provided an incredible sense of exhilaration — the act of doing something forbidden, something dangerous, and getting away with it was fun. Of course, I knew that it was wrong to steal, but it didn't seem like I was hurting anyone. I may have been mistaken about this, but that's how I thought about it at the time.

I'm not embarrassed to admit that I was a shoplifter. Statistically speaking, most of the people reading this will have stolen something at some point in their lives. Shoplifting is an entirely normal thing for a child to do; in fact, I can't help but feel that people who have never stolen anything are a bit odd. I'm not condoning stealing, but I have absolutely no doubt that most children who shoplift are neither 'bad' nor 'immoral'. Yes, I was a shoplifter, but I was also a generally kind and helpful child who rarely behaved in spiteful or malicious ways (I'd like to claim that I never did, but that probably wouldn't be true). Like most children who shoplift, I have not grown up to be a criminal or, I like to think, an otherwise immoral adult.

My friends and I were a competitive bunch, and this extended to shoplifting. We often dared each other to steal things when we were in the shopping centre or at the local street market. Once, acting on such a dare, I stole a three-litre bottle of Coke from a supermarket — an impressive feat if you consider that the bottle was close to half the size of me at the time. On another occasion, I stole ice-cream from under the nose of a street vendor. It was a hot summer's day, and he was selling from a large, refrigerated chest that opened at the top. Being so small, I had to pretty much climb into the fridge in order to see what ice-creams he had. While I was hanging over the edge of it, pretending to rummage around for the one I wanted, I shoved several ice-creams into my jacket. Even today, I have to admit it makes me smile to remember how casually I dropped back down, told the guy that he didn't have what I wanted, and sauntered away with a couple of freezing choc-ices and a Cornetto pressed against my chest.

If you think that this sounds like I was proud of my shoplifting skills, you'd be right. But it was this misplaced pride that landed me in the worst trouble ever. One afternoon after school, a group of friends and I walked to the local shopping centre. As always, we had no money, and all we could do was window-shop. Before long, I was dared to steal an expensive pen from a glass cabinet in a stationery shop. I knew immediately that it was a stupid thing to attempt — this was not a run-of-the-mill, picking-something-up-and-putting-it-in-your-pocket job, but involved taking something in plain view of the shop's staff. Yet my childish pride and desperation to impress my friends defeated my ability to think things through properly. A few minutes later, I was sitting in the shop manager's office, my friends having all run off. I don't know how long I spent in the office and I don't remember what he said to me, but I do remember begging him not to call my dad. Which, of course, he did.

My father didn't come to pick me up. Instead, he sent Kalidas Hazra, a young man from Bangladesh who was lodging with us while he studied for his master's degree. Kalidas was not like the other Bangladeshis I knew: not only was he from the capital, Dhaka (the rest of us were from Sylhet), he was also Hindu and a vegetarian, and spoke *shudo basha*, the 'proper' way to speak Bangla, which sounded much more posh to us than the dialect we spoke.

As well as being our lodger for a short while, Kalidas also gave lessons in Bangla to me, my siblings, and some of our neighbours' children. We called him 'master sahib', a respectful term for 'teacher', and quickly grew fond of him. In sharp contrast to the imams who were supposed to teach us Arabic at the mosque, he was a patient and caring teacher. He seemed to be from another world to the rest of us — he was much kinder, gentler, and more sensitive than the other Bangladeshi men we knew. Like the imams, he had our parents' permission to beat us, but he only ever hit a child once, even then barely striking the boy on his palm with a ruler while blinking away tears. It was a sight that moved all of us in the class. If I'd had to choose a moral role model from all of the Bangladeshi men I knew as a child, it would have been Kalidas. Ironically, he was the only one who wasn't Muslim.

Kalidas didn't tell me off when he saw me. I think he understood that shoplifting is just one of those things that kids do. Or perhaps he was too kind to add to the misery of a child who was about to be punished so severely. We walked home in silence, sharing an unspoken understanding that neither of us could stop what was going to happen when I got home. I was a dead man walking, and we both knew it.

As soon as I came in the door, my father grabbed me by the hair and started whipping me with his belt. He continued to thrash me as I lay on the floor, in the foetal position, trying to protect myself. He was in such a rage that my mother, Kalidas, and my siblings just stood by in shock, not daring to intercede. I remember my father shouting and swearing at me, his eyes bulging out, spit flying everywhere. And I remember, even as I was in pain from the beating, a sense of surprise as I noticed that I had wet myself.

It might be hard to believe, but I wasn't angry or upset at my father for beating me. I knew that shoplifting was wrong, I knew that I had brought shame on my father and the family, and I knew that I deserved to be punished. So, as my father beat me, I didn't beg him to stop and I didn't make any excuses; I just waited for him to be done.

The next day at school, I was summoned to see the headmaster. I had never dreaded going to see him before. In fact, until this time, I had always enjoyed my visits to Mr Grimmett's office. As well as the official meetings we had for progress checks and so on, he often called on me for help as a translator when he had to deal with Bangladeshi parents. I loved spending time with this wonderfully warm and funny man who had always made me feel special.

I don't know what I was expecting, but what happened couldn't have been a severer punishment. Mr Grimmett looked sad. He stared up at me as I entered his room and said, 'Why, Alom, why?' I don't remember what else he said, but I do know that he didn't shout or tell me off, as I might have expected. Instead, his disappointment washed over me in waves, eliciting the remorse that my father's belt had failed to.

Mr Grimmett and my father were both authority figures in my childhood, but each had a very different influence as far as my behaviour was concerned. I don't think that being beaten by my dad had any effect on the development of my morality. It just made me want to avoid beatings. The easiest way to do that was to avoid getting caught doing things for which I might be beaten ... which did not necessarily mean that I stopped doing those things, just that I took extra care not to get caught.

Mr Grimmett, along with Kalidas and my mother, had a more significant effect when it came to shaping the morality by which I live my life. They were all adults whom I liked — indeed, loved — and respected, and they showed me how to be good through their actions.

I guess God, or Allah, was also an authority figure who should have influenced my behaviour. Like many children, I was brought up with the notion that there is an invisible, all-seeing, all-knowing, all-powerful supernatural being who would reward me if I was 'good' and punish me if I was 'bad'. There was surely a period in my childhood where I believed this, but it was clearly not something I really believed by the time I was shoplifting, or bunking off from the mosque, or secretly trying my father's cigarettes and whisky — all things that were no doubt 'bad' in the eyes of God.

Despite not believing in God, and not believing in an after-life where I might be rewarded or punished for my behaviour, I try to be a good person. That's the most any of us can do. But I don't believe that anyone is entirely 'good'. Even histori-cal figures admired by millions of people for their good works did things that were morally dubious — there's evidence that Martin Luther King, Jr, plagiarised others in his PhD thesis, for example, and someone who knew Gandhi once described him as 'a most dangerous, semi-repressed sex maniac'.[1]

Mother Teresa was a figure who embodied the notion of goodness to millions of people around the world. Although the Catholic Church has yet to officially declare her a saint, she was often revered as one while she was alive. However, many people, including me, found some aspects of her life and work to be the very opposite of what we would describe as good. Perversely, she seemed to believe that suffering was a virtue, and there is evidence that she willingly let children remain ill and die, despite having the financial resources to help them recover. There is also evidence to suggest that, instead of building the hospitals for which people gave her money, she built convents because she believed that it was more important to increase the number of Catholics in the world than to alleviate the suffering of the poor and the sick. Writer Christopher Hitchens, who met Mother Teresa and investigated her work, concluded in the documentary film *Hell's Angel* that she was 'corrupt, nasty, cynical, and cruel'.[2]

Mother Teresa is an interesting example of someone who led a supposedly pious life and yet behaved in a way that many people would consider immoral. Instead of using her position of enormous power and wealth to help living people, she sought to glorify her God and, let's face it, herself. There are more obvious examples of such contradictory figures: the thousands of Catholic priests found guilty of sexually abusing children, for example, or the evangelists of all religious persuasions who preach the virtues of a wholesome, sinless life while privately leading lives filled with hedonism and debauchery. There were hypocrites like these in my community as I was growing up, including imams who seemed to be bitter and spiteful, taking money from people who couldn't afford it, and delighting in punishing children for the slightest infractions.

While Mother Teresa was, in my opinion, immoral despite her belief in Catholicism, some people would argue that she was a better person, a more moral person, than I am simply because I do not believe in God. Such people believe that you cannot truly be good if you do not believe in Him, that lacking belief is itself immoral and the greatest of all sins. To these people, God is the ultimate source of all morality; they might even claim that the existence of morality is itself proof of the existence of God because if there was no God, there would be no reason to be good. In Dostoevsky's novel *The Brothers Karamazov*, Ivan Karamazov says, 'Without God, everything is permitted.' Others have paraphrased this idea more bluntly: 'If there is no God, I am free to rape my neighbour.'[3]

There is a surprising twist to this type of thinking that may be problematic to even the most devout of believers. It is a question that I suspect many bright children ask themselves at one point or another: is something morally good because God approves of it, or does God approve of it because it is morally good? For example, is murder an intrinsically bad thing, or is it bad because God says it is? And if it's bad because God says it is, could murdering people be considered good if God said it was? This is known as the Euthyphro dilemma, so named because it first appears in Plato's dialogue *Euthyphro*. This dilemma is problematic for people who believe in an all-powerful God because it requires you to believe one of two things: either morality is defined by that which God deems moral and therefore what is good or evil is arbitrary, or morals exist outside of God's will, and so God Himself is bound by laws which He is not responsible for, thus contradicting the idea of an omnipotent god. Either way, you're left with an uncomfortable conclusion about the nature of God.

There is another problem when it comes to God and morality. A friend of mine was struck by this in 2005, a few days after a major earthquake hit Pakistan. We were talking about the horror of the disaster — it had killed tens of thousands, and left millions homeless. He commented, 'I don't understand how an earthquake could happen in Pakistan; it's a Muslim country.' I was astonished, but tried not to show it. There was no faulting his logic — after all, if you believe that everything happens because Allah wills it, and if you believe that Islam is the one true religion, Muslim countries should indeed be safe from natural disasters. Surely Allah would punish the heathen Americans, or British, or Australians with events such as earthquakes before inflicting them on Pakistan, a country full of Muslims?

I could have explained that earthquakes happen for reasons that are well understood by scientists, that they have nothing to do with anything supernatural and everything to do with the physical structure of the Earth, and that they have no connection to the morality of the people who are affected by them. I could have pointed out the injustice of babies being killed in the earthquake, or in fact in any natural disaster — they're only babies; what could they have done to deserve such treatment? I could have extended the logic further, asked my friend why Allah lets some children be born with deformities or disabilities that make their lives painful and difficult. I could have asked him to explain why, if Allah is supposed to be omnipotent, he doesn't intervene when bad things happen to good people. But, not wishing to make him uncomfortable, I did none of these things. I just agreed with him about how terrible the earthquake was.

My friend was expressing something that has bothered millions of other religious people, a theological dilemma known as the problem of evil: if there is a loving, omniscient, omnipotent God, why is there so much evil and suffering in the world? It is thought to be Greek philosopher Epicurus who summed up the problem eloquently, like this:

> Is God willing to prevent evil, but not able? Then he is impotent.
> Is he able but not willing? Then he is malevolent.
> Is he both able and willing? Then whence came evil?
> Is he neither able nor willing? Then why call him God? [4]

The problem of evil genuinely stumps most ordinary believers. In my experience, they usually respond with an answer along the lines of, 'God moves in mysterious ways.' Sometimes they'll say, 'Suffering is God's way of testing us,' to which the obvious response is, 'Why does he have to test us in such evil ways?' To which the response is, 'God moves in mysterious ways.' You get the idea.

Theologians have grappled with the problem of evil and come up with one or two slightly better answers, including the idea that evil is a consequence of God giving us free will (known as the free-will defence). This explains moral evil — actions by humans that cause suffering — but it fails to explain 'natural evil'; that is, suffering caused by disasters and diseases such as earthquakes, floods, and AIDS. In the past, theologians have tried to blame these on humans, too, arguing that they are the consequence of human immorality, punishment from God for sins. AIDS, for example, is sometimes referred to as a 'plague from God'. But this just seems unfair — why would God punish everybody, 'good' and 'bad', within a certain geographic location or social group? There is something about this that grates with our sense of morality. Surely only a sociopath would think it wasn't a problem that innocent people were being made to suffer. So, is God a sociopath?

This idea that disease or misfortune are punishments from God is a pernicious one but, unfortunately, it is one that many theists believe. Shortly after my mother died, I was confronted with just how obnoxious and vile these beliefs can be. While I was hanging around after playing football one afternoon, an older Bangladeshi boy, who had just found out that my youngest brother was disabled, decided to share his deep theological knowledge with me and tell me that my mother's death and my brother's disabilities were proof that God thought there was something rotten with my family. He argued that Allah didn't let these things happen for no reason, so these misfortunes were clearly Allah's will, events to punish my family. Thankfully, some of the other older boys told him to shut up, but I remember feeling like I'd been kicked in the stomach.

My brother is disabled because he was born prematurely and because my mother was ill when she was pregnant with him; this is all the explanation I need. However, like the boy who saw misfortune as some kind of justice, there are many religious people who believe that disability is a form of divine punishment for sins either in this life, or in previous ones. To me, this is a disgusting, immoral way to view people with disabilities, and yet it is a perfectly rational conclusion to arrive at if you believe that God is responsible for the way the world is.

It seems to me that the problem of evil is insurmountable for theists, be they theologians capable of intellectual gymnastics or ordinary believers who don't spend much time thinking about these things. It is hard not to look at all the suffering and evil in the world and avoid the conclusion that God doesn't exist — or, if He does, as Depeche Mode put it, He's got 'a sick sense of humour'.[5]

Yet, despite the logical difficulties presented by the problem of evil, many theists find it impossible to separate their ideas about morality from their religious beliefs. For such people, being good is something that they need to do in order to please God so that they can go to heaven when they die. Luckily for them, most religions come with instructions on how to behave so that they don't displease God or their gods. Perhaps the most famous of such instructions are the Ten Commandments of the Old Testament. Roughly translated, they are:

1. You must only worship the God of the Bible and no other.
2. You must not worship statues or other objects.

3. You must not use the name of God improperly or without respect.

4. You must spend the seventh day of the week doing no work, but thinking about and worshipping God.

5. You must respect your parents.

6. You must not commit murder.

7. You must not commit adultery.

8. You must not steal.

9. You must not lie.

10. You must not desire other people's things.

The first four are about how you should behave in relation to God. Note that breaking any of these would not result in harm to any living thing. The first commandment is an odd one because it implies the existence of other gods. My knowledge of religious history is limited, but I know that at the time these commandments were written, the idea that there was only one god was not as widely accepted as it is today, and so the first commandment was a clever way to get Moses' followers to stop 'believing' in other gods — a marketing ploy rather than a moral imperative. Commandment five might be a tough one if you have abusive or negligent parents. Breaking commandment ten doesn't seem to be something that would necessarily hurt anyone except yourself, but it might make you a happier person if you stuck to it.

According to the story of the Ten Commandments — and, of course, there is no evidence that it is anything more than a story — the commandments were presented to Moses on stone tablets by the one true God. Now, even if, like me, you don't believe in God, you have to at least concede that Moses was pretty clever in telling his followers that the commandments came from God — claiming that the rules you want people to obey come from a higher authority is a useful way to ensure that those rules are followed. It's a strategy that religious leaders have used long before Moses, and it's one that they continue to use today.

Moral guidelines for those who follow the Abrahamic religions have incorporated the Ten Commandments since Old Testament times, but there are a whole host of other rules and regulations with supposed divine authority that Muslims, Jews, and Christians have had thrust upon them in the name of being good. Many Muslims around the world, for example, have their lives governed by Sharia law, which is based on the Qur'an and lays down some incredibly strict guidelines for how to live in a manner that would please Allah. Growing up, I wasn't really aware that Sharia law existed, as my community was not one that adhered strongly to it, but I knew of lots of things I had to do because Allah wanted it that way, including the rule that I must never eat bacon. Like many of the rules that religions would have us follow, it was invented for those living in a different culture — in a different era — and it verges on the ridiculous to think that they should govern us today.

As well as forbidding the eating of pork, there are rules that dictate the kind of meat that Muslims and Jews are allowed to eat — rules that can be considered not only anachronistic but also cruel. Both religions require animals' throats to be slashed while they are still conscious, and the bodies left for the blood to drain out. The animals may remain conscious for some time while the blood leaks away. In both religions, the people doing the throat-slashing are required to utter certain prayers while they do their job but, unfortunately, this does nothing to ease the pain that the animals feel when they are killed in this way. Scientists believe that these animals may suffer considerable pain and distress.[6] Today, when we have many methods to keep meat fresh and free from disease, there is no reason to put animals through this barbaric method of slaughter. In fact, it is illegal in many countries around the world — and yet billions of people insist that the meat they eat is killed in this way. I suspect that, even if we could provide incontrovertible evidence that slaughtering animals in this way caused them unnecessary and avoidable pain, many Jews and Muslims would carry on with this practice. Religion allows people to ignore the needs of real beings in favour of the supposed wishes of a being that does not exist.

But it's not just animals that suffer as a result of people following anachronistic rules and regulations because their religion demands it. There is much human suffering, too, that has its roots in unquestioning adherence to 'divine' commandments. Various passages in the Bible and the Qur'an seem to sanction things such as polygamy and slavery, and demand the killing of non-believers, homosexuals, and even women who fail to prove their virginity on their wedding night.[7] It's one thing to be complicit in the unnecessary suffering of animals; it's another thing entirely to suffer from sexual repression because you've been brought up to believe that God disapproves of masturbation, or to live as a second-class citizen because you're a woman, or to live in fear for your life because you're homosexual. Yet this is the reality that is imposed on millions, if not billions, of people around the world because they live in communities or countries that base their morality and laws on religious beliefs founded on ancient books and stories.

I can't help but think that the Ten Commandments are more than a little poor as a list of ways to be good and that, with a little imagination, most of us could come up with a better one. I'm not going to try to construct such a list here, but if I did, I suspect I'd include references to how we should treat animals, how we should help to protect the environment, and how we should treat humans who are different from ourselves. I'd probably borrow ideas from the Universal Declaration of Human Rights, which states: 'All human beings are born free and equal in dignity and rights. They are endowed with reason and conscience and should act towards one another in a spirit of brotherhood.'[8] Sadly, we live in a world where people's religion can prevent them from believing that all humans are equal. It is an inescapable fact that some religions promote the idea that some humans — for example, homosexuals and women — are somehow inferior to others.

Like billions of other people, I was brought up to believe in hell, a place where I would be made to burn and subjected to terrible torture if I did not behave as I was supposed to. Hell is an incredibly frightening idea to most children, and I was probably scared of it until I stopped believing in it. It's one of those things that make me question how religious people can truly hold their beliefs — if anyone really believed in hell, wouldn't they lead a morally impeccable life?

There is another problematic aspect of hell, one that poses a fundamental problem when it comes to the contemporary conception of God: what kind of loving God would let any of his 'children' suffer for eternity in hell, regardless of what they had done? We punish people on Earth by locking them up in prison, but only a minority of criminals get life sentences — these are reserved for only the most severe and heinous of crimes. Judicial corporal punishment is outlawed in most countries in the western world; by and large, we do not physically punish anyone, regardless of what they have done. Yet, according to some interpretations of Christianity, you can end up burning in hell for eternity even if you lead a 'good' life in all respects, but fail to acknowledge the idea that Jesus is the son of God and that he died on a cross to absolve you of your sins. This is no exaggeration — a strict interpretation of Christian theology insists that you must absolutely buy into this belief or you cannot and will not enter the Kingdom of Heaven. This is a central tenet of Christianity, supported by Jesus' own words, as recorded in the New Testament, in John 14:6: 'I am the way and the truth and the life. No one comes to the Father except through me.'[9] If anyone's motive for 'being good' is a fear of hell or a desire to get into heaven, I can't help but feel that such a person is perhaps not as 'good' as someone who behaves decently towards others for the sake of it and nothing more.

Yet the biggest problem with basing our morality on what we believe a god wants — assuming we believe in the first place that such a being exists — is quite simple: there is no way of knowing conclusively what he, she, or it wants. Only a tiny minority of theists would claim to have direct contact with a god and to know what their god wants. In other words, religious people do not usually get their moral guidance directly from their god, but from other human beings who claim to be speaking on behalf of that god. Essentially, they are basing their morality on others' claims of having visions, and others' interpretations of ancient texts.

The belief that your own religion is the absolute moral truth is a dangerous one. The idea that holy books contain unquestionable moral truths has been abused by authoritarian religious leaders in order to oppress and kill countless numbers of people. A quick glance at the history books reveals just how many wars have been carried out in the name of God. Even as I am writing, there are conflicts spurred by religion that are being waged around the world — for example, as Christians and Muslims clash in various parts of Africa, and Sunni Muslims fight Shi'ites in the Middle East. And all of these people believe that they are being moral, acting in accordance with the wishes of the same God of Abraham.

Some people would go further than me and claim that religion itself is immoral because it holds back the progress of entire societies, stifling scientific and artistic developments with anachronistic rules and regulations. Surely it is immoral to prevent humans from being all they can be? While I wouldn't necessarily agree that religion is morally wrong, it bothers me that so much of it seems to be about keeping people in their places. Just take a look at a country like Saudi Arabia, purportedly an Islamic state that is supposed to be governed by Islamic laws: it doesn't take much investigation to reveal that the ruling royals blatantly flout every Islamic law worth its name — from drinking alcohol to having sex outside marriage — while insisting on severe punishments for ordinary citizens who do the same.

Philosophers, theologians, and all sorts of other thinkers have tried to define the principles of 'goodness'. While there are certain things they may all agree on, ultimately it seems to me that all we have are our own notions of what we will do in particular circumstances, and that our actions will be determined by a range of factors, including our beliefs, experiences, and biological predispositions. As Kenan Malik puts it, 'Moral values do not come prepackaged from God, but have to be worked out by human beings through a combination of empathy, reasoning and dialogue.'[10] To claim that our moral values come from a higher power is to denigrate human goodness and to abdicate responsibility for our actions to an imaginary being. Surely this is itself the most immoral act we can commit as intelligent, compassionate individuals with the capacity and the desire to improve the world?

There are some things that become part of our moral code as we become more knowledgable and learn to see the world in different ways. Morality changes and evolves alongside humans and the societies we live in. Less than 200 years ago, keeping slaves was considered normal, and some people would not have thought it remotely wrong to mistreat them. Yet today we look back on slavery as a barbaric, immoral practice. I suspect that the same may one day be true of meat-eaters like me; I think that the way we treat animals today, particularly the industrialised processes for producing meat and dairy products, will be looked back upon by our descendants as unbelievably savage, and that today's vegetarians will be remembered as moral progressives.

Scientific evidence points to the fact that our morality is a product of our biology and our evolutionary history, and research suggests that we are all endowed with a moral faculty that guides our intuitive judgments of right and wrong.[11] It is likely that the tendency to morality is a basic part of our nature — humans may be naturally disposed towards certain types of moral behaviour, such as not killing, stealing from, or raping those they care about — and that religion simply provides us with an easy way to express and share it. There is no need to invoke the existence of God to explain why humans are moral creatures. I, like the primatologist Frans de Waal, 'have never seen convincing evidence that a belief in

God keeps people from immoral behavior', and I don't feel less moral for not believing in God.[12]

Atheism does not claim to make you a better person, and in that sense it is something that no religion is: honest. It offers a way of life during which we are not forced to feel guilt or shame for things that no human being should feel guilt or shame about, such as our sexuality or our gender, and insists that we take responsibility for our own morality. A lot of religious people struggle with the idea that you can be good without believing in God. But there is no evidence to suggest that atheists commit more crime, violence, or other acts of 'evil' than people who believe in God.

None of us is infallible — we all have our moments of being mean, telling lies, and feeling schadenfreude. If we're honest with ourselves, most of us can identify times when we have treated others unjustly or have unnecessarily caused pain. But I'm not a cynic; I believe that most of us at least aspire to lead moral lives. Perhaps I'm wrong about this, but I'm certain about one thing: slavishly following the words of long-dead men in books that bear little relevance to our contemporary world is no way to truly go about being good.

THREE

ESCAPE TO NARNIA

I ONCE MET a Texan who bragged that he had only ever read one book from cover to cover: the Bible. We met on a walking tour at Volcán de Fuego, a volcano near the Guatemalan town of Antigua. I was there working as a volunteer at a school, and this man and his wife were in the country to adopt a child because God had apparently told them to. They were interesting people — the first I had met who seemed to confirm everything I'd heard about the beliefs of religious fundamentalists from the United States.

The man had taken an interest in me because, with my brown skin and scruffy clothes, I looked like a native but spoke with an English accent. Our conversation had gotten off to a shaky start. Once he found out that I was a science teacher, he said, 'I suppose you're one of those atheists, then.' I consented, but we carried on talking. By the end of the trip, we had become friends. He and his wife invited me back to their home in Texas with a promise to take me deer hunting and to cook 'the best bar-bay-cue you'll ever taste'.

I could understand why this man and his wife held the beliefs they did. They had both grown up in a community where their religion was central to their culture and identity. But there was one thing with which I really struggled to empathise — his pride in having only read one book. He had wanted me to be impressed, but how could I feel anything but pity for a man who had never done what I had: sat with Scout watching her father defend Tom Robinson; fallen in love, as Pip did, with Estella; and stepped through the wardrobe with Lucy?

I love books. They are central to my life. They have shaped me and they have saved me. If loneliness, depression, and fear threaten to overwhelm me, or if I want to escape from the world, where others might turn to drink or drugs, I turn to books. My hunger for them is insatiable. I gorge, usually having two or more on the go at the same time. I seek out intellectual nourishment in 'serious' novels and non-fiction, devour junk in the form of guiltily purchased thrillers, or get a quick literary fix from a comic. I read in bed, on the bus, in the bath, and on the toilet. My soul becomes malnourished if I go without a good book for too long. I am incredibly thankful that there are so many of them, but at the same time disappointed that I will not have enough time in my life to read all the good ones.

When I was a child, books gave me the means to escape my life by entering fictional worlds. I had little idea that they were giving me a practical means to escape the limitations of my circumstances by introducing me to new ideas and new ways of looking at the world. Books gave me what the writer Cory Doctorow describes as 'a whole cognitive and philosophical toolkit for unpicking the world, making sense of its inexplicable moving parts, from people to institutions'.[1]

A friend of mine, an incredibly bright chap who I imagine is far more capable than me of writing a book, once told me that he loved books too much to attempt to write one. It's a comment that has haunted me and left me with a slight sense of shame as I try to write my own. In fact, writing about my love of books is almost harder than writing about how much I loved my mum. So many people love books that I can't help but fail to be sufficiently eloquent about them.

My mother taught me to believe that all books are sacred. She told me that it was a sin to step on a book, or even to step over one on the floor. Should you commit either crime, you were to seek forgiveness by picking up the book, kissing it, touching it to your forehead, and pressing it to your chest. On the occasions when I step on one of the many books strewn over my floor, I still enact this little ritual.

My respect for books may have come from my mother, but it was my father who first taught me to read. I have a vague memory — one of those that is, more than anything, a recollection of a feeling: I am sitting on his lap and turning the pages of one of those alphabet books that can generally be found in even the most deprived of households. It is my fondest memory of my father, regardless of its indistinct nature. It is almost the only time I can remember him doing any of those nice things that a parent is supposed to do. But I am forever grateful to him for it because I remember feeling that reading was incredibly special, and something that pleased my father — for the shortest of times during those moments, I was my father's little boy, and I wanted to impress him. I'm sure that this contributed to my desire to read in those early years.

My father did a good job — when I first started school, the teachers were impressed by my reading and writing skills. I was unusually literate for any child from the estate, not just for a Bangladeshi one.

According to a study carried out by the United States Department of Education in the 1990s, the number of books in a child's home correlates strongly with his or her academic achievement. In other words, a child who is born into a household with a lot of books is likely to do well at school.[2] I grew up in a house with no more than a handful of books: the alphabet book of my early childhood, the Qur'an, and a couple of other religious texts belonging to my mother. But I bucked the trend of these particular statistics because, perhaps from my father's efforts to develop in me a love of reading, I spent almost as many hours in the local library as I did on the football pitch.

I was about five or six years old when I joined the library, after being introduced to it by an older boy who lived on same estate as me. He was intellectually slower than the boys his own age and they bullied him, so he used to hang out with us younger children and bully us instead. We didn't really like him, but he was fun and partly responsible for many of the things I did as a child that my mother would have disapproved of, had she found out. He took me to the library because he'd discovered there were books with photographs of cars, motorbikes, and planes that he could take home. He'd also found a book about pregnancy that had a picture of a woman's breasts in it. Much to his disappointment, I became more interested in the books with stories. He was angry about this, and even hit me over it once, but it was a price worth paying for the joys and privileges that membership of a public library would bring me.

For the first few years after we had arrived in the United Kingdom, we didn't have a television and I didn't have many toys. So when I was introduced to the library, I suddenly found all the entertainment I could want. As well as books, there were board games, toys, and art-and-craft facilities. The staff were wonderful, happy to help me with all of these activities and to find the books I was looking for. They were also keen to recommend other books that they thought I would like. In those days, long before electronic administration systems were in place, the library issued members with little cardboard folders, library 'tickets'. They would take a card from the book you wanted to borrow and file it away in an open-topped wooden tray at the front desk. As a new member, you were only given two tickets. There was a waiting period before you were allowed more, but the librarians, seeing how quickly I got through the books I borrowed, soon gave me the maximum number of tickets and, ignoring the rules, allowed me to use the adult section because I had so rapidly made my way through most of the children's classics.

And perhaps most wonderfully of all, thanks to the presence of the librarians, there was never the danger of a bunch of white kids coming in and starting a fight, or even just telling us to get out. (Although only the nice white kids came to the library, anyway.)

Sadly, in my late teens, soon after we had moved away to Camberwell, things changed for the worse on the estate. The library was set on fire a couple of times. Although I no longer used it, I hated the kids who did this. To me, it was a sacrilegious act. As was the local council's decision, a few years later, to demolish the library and use the land as a car park. Today, a cheap and ugly block of flats stands where my favourite building used to be, and the nearest library is a long walk away for children living in the neighbourhood. Yet although this library no longer exists, the passion for reading that it helped to instil in me will remain until I die.

These days, I buy most of the books I read — not just because I can afford to, but because I feel that buying books, in a small way, helps to keep people writing them. I am glad to pay for the privilege of reading a book, and feel that the few pounds I spend on one is my personal thank-you to the person who wrote it. I now have a small library of my own filled with books I love, books I hope to share with as-yet-unborn nephews and nieces and perhaps even, one day, children of my own.

I have a special affection for certain characters from literature, and I enjoy re-reading books so that I can spend time
with them again. For example, about once a year I re-read *To
Kill a Mockingbird*; I love being in that world, hanging out with
Scout, Jem, and Dill. I've repeatedly returned to *Middlemarch*,
Great Expectations, *Watership Down*, *One Day in the Life of Ivan
Denisovich*, *Watchmen*, and *An Inspector Calls*, and to the adventures of Tom Sawyer and Huckleberry Finn and numerous
other fictional characters. But my favourite book of all time
is Cynthia Voigt's *Homecoming*, which tells the story of four
siblings who traipse across America to find their grandmother
after their mother deserts them and (spoiler alert) later dies.
The story resonated with me for obvious reasons, as my siblings and I were pretty much left to cope alone when my
mother died, but I love the book for more than that: I love it
because it is well written with believable, likeable characters
and a compelling story. A friend of mine jokes that I am in
love with Dicey, the eldest girl, who effectively becomes a
mother to her younger siblings. The thing is, I do love Dicey,
because it is perfectly possible to love a fictional character.

Yet the books with which I have had the longest running
love affair are C.S. Lewis' *The Chronicles of Narnia*. They were
the first books I owned, the first I read repeatedly, and the
first into which I really remember escaping. I wished that
Narnia was real and that I would somehow end up there, and
when things at home were particularly awful I would lie
awake at night, close my eyes, and pray I'd be in Narnia
when I opened them. In Narnia, life was straightforward.

There were problems to be solved, battles to be fought, and enemies to be defeated, but I knew that I could solve the problems, win the battles, and, eventually, defeat the enemies. Fighting monsters seemed like something that I could accomplish. What I felt helpless to do anything about were the real problems that plagued me: I could not change the fact that my mother was ill, and I could not stop my father from drinking or gambling or being mean to my mother and us kids. I've been told more than once that I have a hero complex, that I want to save everyone. But how can you read these stories and not develop one? Who doesn't want to be a hero?

I have lost count of the number of times I have read some of the chronicles, but I remember clearly that I was 16 when someone told me that they were allegories for Christianity. I was one of a number of students working a Saturday shift in the catering department at the National Theatre. It was a slow day; I was on till duty and I had a copy of *The Lion, The Witch and The Wardrobe* in my lap, which I was trying to read surreptitiously in the long gaps between customers. One of my colleagues, one of the few older people who worked there, noticed the title and said casually, 'You know that's all about Jesus, right?'

I didn't know. The references to Christian mythology had been lost on me as a child and a teenager, as I imagine they are lost on most younger readers. But as soon as it was pointed out to me, the penny dropped, and I was left stunned by how obvious the whole Aslan-as-Christ thing was.

Thinking about it later, as I continued to read the book on my bus journey home, I realised I was disappointed. I felt deceived by Lewis. And sad, because I knew that Lewis would never have imagined someone like me to be a Narnian. It pains me to say it, even now, but I suspect that he would have been a bit of a racist. Lewis would not have envisioned me fighting alongside Lucy and her siblings as one of Aslan's army; he'd have seen me as a savage from the land of Calormen, on the side of the horrendous bird-headed demon-god Tash.

Despite this, I still go back and re-read the books. I'm perfectly capable of ignoring Lewis' attempts at proselytising while enjoying the adventures of the Pevensie children and their friends. I still think Lewis was an incredible writer — the books are rich in imagination, filled with the kind of ideas that make for great reading, pacy, and full of drama. *The Voyage of the Dawn Treader*, perhaps my favourite in the series, contains more adventure in under 200 pages than any number of the multi-volume fantasy epics published today. However, it wouldn't be true to say that my knowledge of the religious overtones hasn't affected my engagement with the books. I have read some of the chronicles more often than others. I don't read *The Magician's Nephew* or *The Horse and His Boy* as often, for example. And I find the seventh book, *The Last Battle*, rather unpleasant towards the end because the story becomes explicitly about religion and lacks even the slightest subtlety in delivering its message of salvation through Christ.

According to George Sayer's biography of C.S. Lewis,

Jack, Lewis admitted that he hoped, through *The Chronicles of Narnia*, to 'make it easier for children to accept Christianity when they met it later in life', describing his work as 'a sort of pre-baptism of the child's imagination'.[3] Apparently he was quite successful — there seem to be many who credit these books with converting them to Christianity in their early years, or with strengthening their existing belief in Christ. However, Lewis failed to ease my acceptance of any religion or convince me that there was a richer existence to be had in a life after death with God. I didn't particularly like Aslan; I think I found him a little unfriendly, and a bit smug, superior. And I didn't like that he always had to come to the rescue. I always felt that the stories would have been better if the children had solved their problems on their own. Lewis believed that you needed God to get through life whereas, long before I had worked out what Lewis meant, I think I knew that life's problems had to be faced without any kind of divine help, whether from a magical lion or an invisible man in the sky.

Although I didn't know it at the time, Lewis' books were probably my first encounter with religious literature. By the time I was 11, I was having to read the Bible in religious education lessons at school (and being fed extracts from the Qur'an at the local mosque). These stories of God and creation failed to impress me; maybe it was that Genesis is not the most arresting opening chapter, but I wasn't convinced that the stories I heard from it were any different from the other — frankly, more enjoyable — stories I had read. The God of the

Bible seemed surprisingly human for a god, not at all hero-like. And, having been schooled in the fantasy genre from an early age, I couldn't really believe that a being capable of the amazing act of Creation would want something as mundane as having His creations worship and obey Him. Why would a god that powerful care? Why would He be so *human*? I couldn't have expressed it then but, for me, an anthropomorphic god was just too boring and unimaginative. A god created in our own image just didn't ring true. It's a problem I have with all literature — I cannot get along with a book in which the characters and their motivations are unbelievable.

Most children brought up in the Abrahamic religions — Judaism, Christianity, and Islam — are presented at a young age with the figure of God. In most cases, God will be some form of omnipotent, omniscient father figure, an old man with a beard who lives up in the sky, pretty much as Michelangelo depicts God in his painting in the Sistine Chapel. This will often be the figure of God these children believe in for the rest of their lives, as it is presented to them at an age when they haven't yet developed the critical-thinking skills to question and evaluate the existence or non-existence of such a being. One reason why the idea of God is so hard for some people to let go of is that it was planted in their heads at an age when it could take root without resistance.

In the west, children usually encounter other gods — for example, Greek or Norse — either at school or in books. Most happily accept that these gods are fictional, but never stop to ask why the god of their own religion should not be fictional. Most brought up in an Abrahamic religion will grow up with the idea that their god, the God of Abraham and of Moses, is the one true god — the only god that ever existed and the only god that will ever exist. Their sense of superiority about this carries over into adulthood: as others have pointed out, religious people tend to be atheists when it comes to the gods of religions other than their own.[4]

It might surprise some believers in the Abrahamic God to know that, in the early days of Judaism, Christianity, and Islam, supporters of all those religions were once described as 'atheists' by people who did not believe in the God of Abraham. Karen Armstrong, a former Catholic nun, details this in her book *A History of God*, in which she attempts to map out 'the way men and women have perceived [God] from Abraham to the present day'.[5] The book shows that the God of Abraham is not an eternal, unchanging being, but rather an idea that has changed over the two thousand or so years since the stories about Him first started to be told. Armstrong writes that 'there is not one unchanging idea contained in the word "God"... there is no objective view of "God": each generation has to create the image of God that works for them.'[6]

A little reading around the subject reveals that some of the Biblical stories featuring the Abrahamic God are almost certainly loose adaptations of earlier myths. Noah was not the first character in a story who had to deal with a massive flood, and Jesus was not the first to be born when a woman was impregnated by a god. The figure of the Abrahamic God has evolved from earlier gods, and continues to evolve as new interpretations of the Abrahamic religions or, indeed, entirely new religions, spring up. In one sense, and perhaps because I am a reader of comics, it seems much like the way in which every generation has its own take on classic superheroes through new films and books. New movie versions of *Batman*, *Spiderman*, and *Superman* seem to be perpetually in production, giving new writers and directors the opportunity to tell these stories in their own way. (And in another parallel with religion, these different versions of superhero stories lead to endless discussions about which is the most authentic depiction of a particular character.)

It is ironic that religious people think of God as 'eternal', when the evidence from history is clear that our very human ideas about God are anything but immutable.

Stories, myths, and legends are a vital part of human culture. The evidence is that we have a deep psychological need for them; they help us to make sense of the world.[7] They are powerful instruments for communicating our deepest beliefs about the way we believe the world is and the way we think it should be.

So I like to think that I understand why holy books are important: they contain the stories that define the religions to which they belong. They are so powerful *because* they are stories, not just the instruction manuals or reference books that they are often thought to be.

I'm not suggesting that holy books are bereft of wisdom or enlightenment or just plain common sense, either. I think it is important to appreciate that, regardless of what I think of such texts, the majority of the world's population regard some holy book or other as containing fundamental truths about the way the world is and how we should live in it.

However, these books can cause trouble when the boundaries between myths and reality become blurred, and when people start to take them literally. That's when people start to use the myths they hold dear to justify their actions in the real world, including oppressing, or even killing, those who do not share the same beliefs.

Millions of Christians believe that the Bible is the literal word of God. They believe it all, from the story that God made the world in six days to the one about Noah building a boat that carried two of every animal on the planet. Aside from the fact that common sense and science exclude the possibility of either of these things, there is an overwhelming weight of evidence that the Bible was put together over a long period of time by many authors. It was translated from original texts in Aramaic, Hebrew, Greek, and Latin, and subject to much input and interpretation from human sources. The Old and New Testaments are sacred because they represent a kind of agreed consensus about what God is and what He wants of us.

Ironically, and contrary to what many Christians believe, the literal truth of the Bible is not even a central tenet of Christianity. According to author Stephen Tomkins:

Part of the problem is historical. The deification of the Bible is a result of the Protestant reformation. Before then, the final authority, the ultimate arbiter and source of information in religious matters was the church, with its ancient traditions and living experts. When Luther and friends opposed the teaching of the Catholic hierarchy, they needed a superior authority to appeal to, which was provided by the Bible.[8]

Fortunately, many Christians seem happy to accept that the Bible is not the literal word of God. This allows them plenty of room to discuss the meaning of their holy texts and to treat the stories in these books as metaphors or allegories. It permits, even encourages, their religion to reform and evolve along with the rest of society. Instead of being some kind of inerrant document of 'the truth', holy books, according to some Christians (and Jews, for that matter), are simply tools for arriving at the truth for themselves.

Yet, unlike Christian and Jewish doctrines, Islam demands unambiguously that Muslims accept the Qur'an as the word of God. One is not a true Muslim unless he or she accepts that the words in the Qur'an are of divine origin, revealed to Muhammad through the angel Gabriel. This puts the Qur'an into an entirely different league as a sacred text. Many Muslims also maintain that the only way to truly engage with the Qur'an is to read it in Arabic: one has not read the Qur'an if he or she has only read a translation.

The belief that the Qur'an is an eternal, immutable text

endows it with a unique level of authority when compared
to any other work of literature — if I can even be allowed
to call it that. There has been no reformation in Islam, and
it doesn't look like there's going to be one any time soon.
There will always be strong resistance to any attempt at reformation because Islam is inflexible in its claim that the
Qur'an is of divine origin. And in this sense, Islamic funda-
mentalism seems almost understandable, for how can you
not be a fundamentalist if you have the word of God at your
disposal? If you believe the Qur'an to be the word of God,
it would be irrational not to follow its every instruction —
and reason and science must, by definition, concede
authority to it.

I'm certainly not qualified to provide a detailed critique of
either the Bible or the Qur'an. But I have at least made the
effort to read them. I find it astonishing and depressing that
many people who lead their lives according to the ideas and
rules laid down in these books have not read them. I once
asked a young Muslim how she knew that the Qur'an was
true. She replied that the writing in the Qur'an was so beautiful that it could not possibly have been written by a human.
I was flabbergasted by this argument, and could not come up
with a suitable response. I felt that it would be rude to contradict her by pointing out that I knew that her knowledge of
literature was limited to a handful of books, so it was unlikely
she was qualified to accurately judge the beauty that mortals
were capable of producing in a work of literature. She had
certainly never read the works of Oscar Wilde, Primo Levi,

or Jhumpa Lahiri, for example, who have all produced magnificently beautiful literature.

To add a further dimension of oddness to her belief about the Qur'an, the girl had not read the Qur'an in any proper sense of the verb 'to read'. She had been brought up, like many Muslims around the world, to 'read' Arabic in the sense of being able to recognise the sounds to which the symbols corresponded and to be able to pronounce the words they formed when combined, but she was not taught what those Arabic words meant. I know this because I was taught to do the same. It is a common practice in non-Arabic-speaking Muslim communities and one that, even as a child, I found baffling.

The English translation of the Qur'an is written in verse, but it is far from poetic, and I have found it rather difficult to read. There are poems written by humans — Louise Glück, Pablo Neruda, and Wendy Cope, to name just a few — that have moved me far more deeply. Perhaps I might find the Qur'an a more satisfying read if I were capable of reading and comprehending it in Arabic. But I suspect that even if I could understand the words, I would not be convinced that it was so beautiful that it must have been of divine origin.

There is no doubt that the Bible, the Qur'an, the Sri Guru Granth Sahib, the Bhagavad Gita, and other religious books hold profound meaning for billions of people. There is no doubt that their stories have the power to resonate deeply. But in my mind, there is also no doubt that they are ultimately books written *by* humans *for* humans. There is no need to believe that they have a divine origin — books, and the ideas they carry, are powerful enough without imbuing them with divine authority. Once we do that, we are in danger of losing the most important thing that books can do for us: make us think. Humans have always struggled with, and will continue to struggle with, questions about how we should live our lives, who we are, and where we come from. To simply accept that these answers have been written down in books that are hundreds or thousands of years old is to stifle human creativity and to ignore our capacity to think for ourselves, to change and evolve.

There is another, perhaps more sinister, danger associated with subscribing to the notion that any one text is the ultimate authority on everything: it allows for the creation of religious institutions to rule over us. The word 'Islam' means 'submission' in Arabic. To some, it means a voluntary submission to Allah's will, but to me it highlights the fact that most religions require people to submit to rules and regulations enforced by other humans, to concede authority to priests and others further up in the religious hierarchy. Even as a child, it seemed to me that the main purpose of religion was to control my behaviour, not to take me closer to God or enhance my 'spirituality'.

It's evident that religions such as Islam and Christianity have been extremely successful in terms of controlling the behaviour of entire societies, and that 'ordinary' believers have always had less power than those who claim to be closer to God. In the past, before literacy was widespread and when the Bible was only available in Greek or Latin, priests and others who could read it were given a higher status in society, a status from which they personally benefited. Even today, when most people in the west can access the words in the Bible for themselves, it continues to be a source of power and authority for those who claim to understand it better. It is similar for Islam: in my own experience, I saw that becoming a religious leader was a pretty good way to ensure a comfortable life, one in which your views would be left unchallenged because you always had the Qur'an on your side, and most of those around you believed that you understood it better than them. As Thomas Paine put it at the end of the eighteenth century, institutionalised religion is 'no more than human inventions, set up to terrify and enslave mankind, and monopolise power and profit'.[9]

Some people also argue that holy books are important because they provide a basis for our morality. Without such books, they suggest, humans would not know how to act morally. Needless to say, this is simply untrue. There are, and have been, many societies that did not have the benefit of a universally accepted sacred text and yet had collective morals. Anthropologists have found such societies even in recent history. For example, the 'lost tribes' found in New Guinea, South America, and Asia have not been influenced by the teachings of the Abrahamic religions, and yet live moral lives not so different from ours. And today, billions of people in secular societies live without seeking moral guidance from any holy book, instead relying on laws founded on the empathy and wisdom of their fellow humans.

The morality presented in the holy books of the major religions is outdated. An honest reading of these books shows them to be sexist, racist, and homophobic, not to mention contradictory. The Bible and Qur'an reinforced the inferior status of women in the times and societies for which they were written. The Qur'an, for example, gives instructions that the testimony of a man in court can only be equalled by that of two women, and that a woman should only receive a half-share of an inheritance compared to a man. One heinous consequence of this kind of attitude towards women is that the Islamic state of Pakistan, until relatively recently, required a rape victim to provide four male witnesses in order to seek punishment for the rapist.[10] Both the Qur'an and Bible have passages that suggest menstruation is 'impure' or 'unclean', and they have been used to justify practical discrimination against women in terms of forbidding them from taking part in collective worship.[11] It seems to me that such passages reinforce the ultimate source of all religious sexism — the story of Adam and Eve, in which it is Eve who is responsible for humanity's fall from paradise. The gay rights campaigner Peter Tatchell has repeatedly challenged religious homophobia, and has said that 'The Bible is to gays what *Mein Kampf* is to Jews.' He has also drawn attention to religious-sanctioned racism, giving as an example 'the way the leaders of the Dutch Reformed Church defended white superiority during the apartheid era in South Africa', and comparing the 'theological justification of racial discrimination against black people' to religious homophobia.[12] And to take just one contradiction: in

Exodus, Moses is said to have been given the Ten Commandments by God, one of which is 'Thou shalt not kill'. But a few
pages later, Moses tells his followers that the 'Lord God of
Israel' has commanded them to go on a killing spree, to 'go in
and out from gate to gate throughout the camp, and slay
every man his brother, and every man his companion, and
every man his neighbour'.[13]

Just because myths have played an important role in shaping societies and their morality in the past does not mean that
they have to do so today. The logic does not follow. I would
be the first to admit that stories can tell us profound truths
about the world and about ourselves, but it saddens me that
so many religious people seem to reject other sources of
knowledge — particularly science, and the insights it gives us
into how humans think, behave, and live — in favour of religious sources. We should acknowledge the fact that humans
are capable of finding out truths for ourselves.

We all like stories where good triumphs over evil, where
the heroes overcome adversity or persecution to live happily
ever after, and we yearn for such narrative completeness in
our own lives. Belief in God promises that there is some way
in which this will happen for us, that we too will be 'rescued',
whether in this life or the next. However, as much as I loved
The Chronicles of Narnia, and as much as I might have wished
to be a Narnian, I have not based my adult life around the
notion that I will one day meet Aslan and live for eternity by
his side. The reality depicted in most holy books is just as
much a work of the human imagination as Narnia. There is

no denying the historical and cultural significance of such books, and we can learn much from studying them. But just as children grow up and relinquish the idea of ever escaping into Narnia, I can't help but feel that humanity as a whole must grow up and let go of some of the ideas that religions and their holy books present us with. A degree of imagination and faith can enrich our lives, but there is a point at which we can be asked to suspend disbelief too far and become susceptible to ideas that are ultimately unhelpful, or even harmful.

A friend of mine, an English teacher, tells me that a good knowledge of the Bible can massively enhance one's appreciation of English literature. But it is not a book I particularly want to re-read, even though I suspect that he's right: it is probably foolish not to read the Bible if you are interested in developing a deep understanding of English literature. In fact, I would even suggest that reading the holy books of the world's major religions is necessary for anyone who wishes to develop an understanding of human culture in general. However, we must resist the inclination to give them a status beyond that which they genuinely deserve. Instead, we should embrace the notion, sacrilegious to some, that there is greater knowledge, deeper wisdom, and more profound truths to be found in other, no less fictional, books.

FOUR

COCONUT

My FRIENDS JOKE that I am a coconut: brown on the outside, but white on the inside. While they may jest, many people use the term 'coconut' as an insult to attack those who they feel have somehow betrayed their race, to shame those who have not complied with an ideal of what a black or brown person should be like. For me, the term has insidious connotations — it implies that the colour of your skin should determine how you behave, what music you enjoy, what types of culture you consume, and which ideas and values you should believe in. The insult has at its heart an idea that is anathema to me: that we are not free to choose who we want to be.

I have to confess that, growing up in a particularly racist neighbourhood in south-east London in the 1970s, part of me really did want to be white. White people seemed to have better, happier, easier lives. The Britain I had arrived in as a three-year-old was very different from the Britain I now love as my home — it was a nation where people like me could expect to encounter violent racism, and words like 'nigger' and 'Paki' were used openly and without shame.

I spent most of my early childhood in Elephant and Castle. Ironically for a place with such an exotic, romantic name, it was notorious for poverty, crime, and violence. When we first moved there in the mid-1970s, the neighbourhood was not a welcoming place for Bangladeshis and other non-white people. The openly racist political party the National Front had many supporters in the area, and the influx of 'dirty foreigners' was met with hatred, bigotry, and abuse. As primary-school children, we were not safe from this prejudice. I was spat at and verbally abused by white people, but I luckily escaped being beaten up. Many of my childhood friends were less fortunate, and some were subjected to gruesome levels of violence involving cricket bats and other improvised weapons. Mostly I ignored this abuse, feeling helpless to do anything, although there was one occasion — perhaps my most heroic moment — when the sense of injustice overcame me and I beat up a white boy who was punching a friend of mine for no reason other than because he was brown.

During much of my childhood, we lived in a council flat, on the second floor of a block which, with two other blocks, formed a square. In the centre of the square, contained in a large rectangular metal cage, was a children's play area, of the sort that can still be found in the middle of council housing estates around the country. Most flats had a pretty good view of it from the front door, and parents living on the higher floors could look down on their children from the communal balconies. To my friends and me, that metal cage was both physically and metaphorically the heart of the housing estate. It was partitioned so that the smaller part of it contained the usual swings and climbing frames for kids to clamber over, but I spent most of my time in the other part — the football pitch. This was simply a large, open space with a metal frame serving as a goal at each end. Yet it was also the stage on which many dramatic moments unfolded, the place where I spent the happiest hours of my childhood — and also some of the saddest.

Of course, on that pitch the usual childhood rivalries and competitiveness were displayed, but there was rarely any genuine unpleasantness between us. On most days, the pitch was joyous, filled with children playing boisterously and happily. Even if there were just two of us, we could spend many happy hours kicking a ball from one end to the other, playing 'goalie to goalie'. If there were more of us, and we got bored with playing regular football, we played something we called 'Chinese football', in which the aim was to kick the ball as hard as possible while trying to hit other players above the knee in order to knock them out of the game. Some of us primary-school children were better footballers than the older kids, so it was not unusual to see pre-teen boys playing alongside adolescents, teens, and even grown men; the barriers of age were cast aside for the thrill of playing against real competition. Anyone looking down at us from one of the surrounding balconies would have been presented with indisputable evidence that football was indeed 'the beautiful game'.

But every once in a while, our childhood idyll would be shattered. We would see a gang of white youths coming towards us and, almost like in a film, silence would fall on the pitch and the ball would come to a stop. Some of the children would run off straight away, while others, like me, would hang around in the hope that maybe this time — just this once — they'd leave us alone.

'Fuck off, Pakis, this is our pitch.'

If we were lucky, the threat of violence would be left to hang in the air while those of us who had remained made our way out, disappointed that once again none of the older Bangladeshi boys had had the guts to stand up for us. If we didn't move quickly enough for them, the white kids would start to push and shove us, throwing in the occasional slap to the head or kick in the shins. None of this hurt as much as the shame of not hitting back.

The white kids who terrorised us didn't live on our estate. They came in from neighbouring, predominantly white estates, or even further afield. The gangs comprised older teens as well as primary-school children, kids that we could have taken on in a fair fight. But a fair fight was never on offer. We knew that these kids weren't on their own — that, unlike other childhood bullies, they had the authority of adults on their side; their parents would approve of and even encourage their actions. These gangs represented the hatred of entire communities of white people, and we knew, from horror stories of racist violence elsewhere, that hitting back would be a short-lived victory.

These kids didn't usually stay long. They didn't really want to play football; they were just bullies wanting to show off their power and revel in our fear of them. We'd watch them from the balconies above, seething with rage. But I felt something in addition to rage: contempt for their poor football skills. I could see that many of us were better footballers than them, and this let me know that they weren't really better than us in any way, even if they acted as if they were.

This kind of intimidation from a group of white kids was one thing — it was a primitive form of flexing their muscles, trying to stir up a turf war and generally behave like bullies. More insidious, to me, was the fact that even grown-ups felt entitled to abuse us, albeit verbally. The sting of the word 'Paki' is one of the indelible memories of my childhood. It was usually shouted at us from across a street, often accompanied by the adjectives 'dirty', 'smelly', or 'fucking'. Sometimes, it was hurled at us with a dollop of spit and a demand that we 'fuck off back' to where we had come from. I was even called 'Paki' by a police officer as he chased a group of us climbing the scaffolding of a derelict building. On one occasion, I was in a shop when a toddler pointed at me and said to her mother, 'Mummy, Paki.'

English was my second language, but I had picked it up quickly once I started school. I loved words, and took great pride in passing vocabulary tests with flying colours. Yet 'Paki' was a word I wished didn't exist. It has its roots as an abbreviation of the word 'Pakistani', but it wasn't used in the same way you might call a British person a 'Brit' or an Australian an 'Aussie'. In my experience, 'Paki' was always used as an expression of racial hatred — anyone saying it always intented to insult and hurt us. 'Paki' was a label thrust upon us by racists — an identity that made us, by definition, inferior beings with an inferior way of life. Hate speech of this sort is genuinely remarkable: somehow, in the mouths of racists, such words can convey, with utter precision, more feelings of hatred and contempt for other human beings than a thousand other words together.

I've since heard people argue that words such as 'Paki' and 'nigger' are 'just words', but they are missing the point. The meaning of these words is deeply imbued with a notion of racial hatred that is hard for some people to imagine, simply because they have never and can never experience such racism for themselves. For example, there is no word that I know of for white people that can make them feel, and indeed believe, that they are inferior by design. Perhaps, given that most history has been written by white people — most often the conquerors, the oppressors, and the enslavers — such a word cannot exist.

Prejudice has not gone away, but it does shift focus. Today, while non-whites may not be subjected to quite the same levels of abuse and discrimination that I was as a child, Muslims around the world are victims of increasing levels of Islamophobia, a form of prejudice based on religion rather than skin colour. In western countries such as Australia, the United

States, and Britain, Islamophobes are easy to find: from Kye
Keating, a young Australian man who organised a 'Ban the
Burqa Day' through Facebook, to the members of the Tea
Party in the United States, who openly describe Islam as a
'dark and dangerous and devious religion' with a 'culture that
keeps hundreds of millions of people right on the edge of
murder and mayhem 24 hours a day', to organisations such as
the English Defence League (EDL) who invite you, on their
Facebook page, to join them if you 'are fed up and sick to the
back teeth of Islamic Extremism'.[1] Supporters of the EDL
have been involved in violent attacks on Muslims, and yet,
with what can only be deliberate perversity, the EDL describes
itself as a 'human rights organisation'.[2]

Islamophobia is by no means a post-9/11 phenomenon. In
1997, the Runnymede Trust issued a report on Islamophobia,
describing it as 'an ugly word for an ugly reality'. The report
went on to summarise the closed views of Islam held by
Islamophobes, including the idea of the religion as 'violent,
aggressive, threatening, supportive of terrorism, engaged in
a clash of civilisations'.[3] However, it is clear that since 9/11
the western media have conspired to create a view of Muslims
that is overwhelmingly negative. As Christopher Allen writes
in the report 'Islamophobia in the Media since September
11th':

> What they have wholeheartedly reinforced is what I would
> suggest is the most dangerous aspect of Islamophobia; that
> Islam is entirely unidimensional and monolithic without

any internal differentiation or opinion. Through indiscriminately saddling stories about Muslims in Afghanistan and Palestine with similar stories of Muslims in Britain, both the press and the wider media have deliberately overlooked the diversity that exists in both the British and global Islamic community. As such, it attributes to all Muslims the entire spectrum of negative characteristics that are fundamental to Islamophobia.[4]

Just as the racists I grew up with saw all brown people as being the same — that is, inferior — Islamophobes today see all Muslims as the same, and completely fail to acknowledge the diversity and differences in values that are held by the millions of Muslims in the world.

You may wonder why, if I no longer identify as Muslim, I care so deeply about this. I could argue that I find racism in any form objectionable, and that Islamophobia concerns me because it is often, as in the case of the EDL, a thinly disguised excuse for giving vent to dangerously racist views. However, there's more to it: I think that it is important for people like me, who are critical of some aspects of Islam, to be clear that our criticisms are not founded on the same racist assumptions, or motivated by the same kind of thinking. We can be critical of the ideology behind Islam, as well as the way in which it is sometimes practised, without being critical of those who believe in Allah or attend a mosque. People often unfairly conflate the two and, as a believer in human rights and justice, I find this abhorrent.

It depresses me that, instead of challenging Islamophobia, substantial sections of the media continue to incite it — even today, more than a decade after 9/11. Sections of the media frequently portray Muslims in a bad light, and print exaggerated or untrue stories in their attempts to promote their undisguisedly prejudicial agenda.[5] British newspaper headlines, for instance, have screamed out about young Muslim 'thugs' burning poppies on Remembrance Day while chanting 'British troops burn in hell!', and it seems that every December there is a 'Mad Mullah' who wants to ban Christmas. In Australia, media outlets reported that Arab-Australians burned the Australian flag at a rally, when in fact it was burned by Anglo-Australian 'anarchists'. And in the United States, Fox News does so little to hide its anti-Muslim agenda that studies have found that 'Americans who most trust Fox News are more likely to believe that Muslims want to establish Shari'a law, have not done enough to oppose extremism, and believe investigating Muslim extremism is a good idea.'[6] While there genuinely is a minority of Islamic fundamentalists who behave in objectionable ways, much media coverage of Muslims serves to create an impression that all followers of Islam are out to destroy the western way of life. It is fearmongering and incitement to hatred at its worse.

The prevalence of Islamophobic attitudes in the media was in particularly stark evidence in July 2011, when several prominent newspapers around the world jumped to the conclusion that Muslim extremists were responsible for the mass murder of 77 people in Norway. The Murdoch-owned British newspaper *The Sun* published the headline 'Al Qaeda Massacre, Norway's 9/11' before there was any evidence to connect the horrific events to Al Qaeda or any other Islamist groups.[7] Even when it became clear that the killings were carried out by Norwegian right-wing extremist Anders Behring Breivik — who described himself as a Christian — *The New York Times* and others continued to try to pin some kind of blame on Muslims by claiming that, even if it wasn't Al Qaeda this time, other extremists and terrorist groups were being influenced by Al Qaeda's actions and were still mimicking 'Al Qaeda's brutality and multiple attacks'.[8]

I had my own encounter with Islamophobia on a train journey in 2005, a short time after the 7 July terrorist attacks in London. A passenger, a white man, who was sitting across the aisle from me caught my eye. He leaned forward to say, 'Can I ask you a question?' He had a can of lager in his hand and reeked of alcohol, but I replied, 'Yeah, sure.' Thinking it would be something innocuous about train lines or stations, I was unprepared for what he said next: 'Why do you people hate us so much?' He said it with an air of sadness, not anger. I knew that by 'you people', he meant 'Muslims', and even though I didn't think of myself as Muslim, I said to him, 'We don't. I'm really sorry you feel that way.' I was worried he would want to take the conversation further, but, much to my relief, he seemed to accept what I said and leaned back in his seat.

I can't help but feel that Islamophobia must, for some people, have the same devastating effect that racism had on me as a child. To me, it is an issue of human rights: I worry that many Muslim people in the west now feel like second-class citizens because of their religion. Although I no longer share their beliefs, and I am critical of many aspects of Islam, the knee-jerk Islamophobia that took hold of the western world following 9/11, and shows no signs of abating, concerns me.

As well as the negative consequences of being treated as 'the enemy', the rise of Islamophobia has had an even more profound effect on many people of Bangladeshi, Pakistani, or Indian descent living in the west — it forces them to think of themselves first and foremost as Muslims, whereas previously they may have identified more closely with their particular cultural or ethnic origins. I've seen the transformation in people I know, and in the communities I have lived and worked in. For many of the people I grew up with, being Muslim is inseparable from being Bangladeshi. The same is true of many of the students I have taught, as evidenced by a conversation I have had on more than one occasion.

Bangladeshi student (clearly excited and a little proud at encountering their first Bangladeshi teacher): 'Are you from Bangladesh, sir?'

Me: 'Yes.'

Student: 'You must be a Muslim, then.'

Me: 'No, I'm an atheist.'

Student (a little bewildered): 'But you're from Bangladesh. You must be a Muslim.'

It is genuinely disconcerting for some students to find that I can be from Bangladesh and yet also be an atheist. Like many young people, they have inherited their sense of identity from their parents and have seen themselves as a set of labels, not necessarily knowing that they have some choice as to which of these labels they choose to accept.

We teach children, from their earliest days, the words that define them: their names, genders, position in the family, and religious affiliations. Like most children, I had very little notion of my 'identity', but I knew that there were things that defined me: I was a boy and not a girl; I had brown skin, not white; and I was supposed to be Muslim. I was quite happy being a boy; but, as for having brown skin and being Muslim, I believed I had no choice in either matter. As my childhood experiences showed me, prejudice can have the insidious effect of making victims question their potential as human beings. Although I am an atheist, I nevertheless find it distressing that people can be contemptuous of all Muslims based on their own prejudices about what it means to be Muslim. Some atheists are guilty of this ideological categorisation, too, and it bothers me that some of those who really should know better feel that Muslims and non-Muslims cannot, by definition, get along. I suspect this is a point on which I differ from many more-hardline atheists, but perhaps my own experience of being judged for my skin colour has made me acutely sensitive to such judgements being exercised upon others.

Despite some of my awful experiences as a child, I still live in pretty much the same neighbourhood; Elephant and Castle is still the place I call home. It's very different today — waves of African, Eastern European, and South American immigrants have all stamped their mark on the area. Many of these immigrants will have had to endure their own experiences of racism, including, sadly, prejudice from the Bangladeshis who were there before them. However, attitudes towards racism have changed since I was a child. It's no longer socially acceptable in most circles to express openly racist sentiments and, although there are occasional spikes, racially motivated violence has decreased overall. In fact, things have improved so much that some people find it hard to imagine that they were really as bad as people like me remember. The word 'nigger' has been reclaimed by some black people (especially, it would appear, as an indispensable part of the vocabulary of hip-hop artists) and the word 'Paki' is often thrown about by people from the Indian subcontinent in jest, or even as a term of endearment. But for me, and I suspect for many others who experienced these words in their traditional, racist context, neither word has lost its power to hurt.

We are all guilty of holding prejudices, but we owe it to ourselves and to society in general to examine and challenge them. As psychologist Dr Dorothy Rowe has written, 'We all want to be the person we know ourselves to be, and for others to recognise this and treat us with respect. We want to live without being dominated by fear, to enjoy good relationships, and to have a secure place in our society.'[9] This is an ideal worth striving for, but it is one that can only be realised if we all accept that there is no single way for a Muslim or a brown person or, for that matter, an atheist, to be.

Being an atheist is an important part of my identity, but this was not always the case. Like many, if not most, young people, I initially accepted the identity that was handed down to me by my parents. I continued to describe and even, to some extent, to think of myself as Muslim until my late teens.

My journey to becoming a fully fledged atheist began at secondary school, where I started to think consciously about my identity for the first time. I attended a private school, the kind that usually only the rich and privileged can afford. This surprises some people at first, and it's a fact that few guess upon meeting me. However, some people have told me that they could tell. Apparently, there are signs for those in the know: privately educated men have a particular type of confidence, even arrogance, that gives them a certain air. I don't know whether that's true or not, but I probably have more than my fair share of self-confidence.

Of course, my parents didn't pay for me to attend Alleyn's. I owe more than money could repay to two teachers who paved the way for me to go there: Bruce Grimmett, my primary-school headmaster, and Phil Cook, my Year Six teacher. It was Mr Grimmett's idea for me to apply for an assisted place at Alleyn's (back then, there was a government scheme in Britain that paid for private-school places for poor students). I'm not sure that, at the age of 11, I even knew there were such things as private schools. Even if I had been aware of them, the sums of money involved would have meant that I would not have dared to dream of going to one. Anyway, I had my heart set on Scott Lidgett, an all-boys school in Bermondsey, London, which had a reputation for being 'hard', and appealed to my juvenile sense of machismo.

A few days after I had handed in the application forms for secondary school, I was called to Mr Grimmett's office, and my life took one of those dramatic turns that, up to that point, I had only ever read about in books. I remember the conversation clearly. Mr Grimmett (I can't bring myself to call him 'Bruce', even after so many years) greeted me in his usual cheery way and invited me to sit down. 'I see you've applied to go to Scott Lidgett.'

'Yes, sir.'

'I don't think that would be the best thing for you. What if I told you there was another, much better school you could go to — would you be interested?'

'Yes, sir.'

'It's a special school, and you'd have to take an exam to get in. Would you be willing to do this?'

'Yes, sir.' (Like most of us at the school, I would have done anything for Mr Grimmett.)

'Good,' he said. 'I'll speak to your father and make the arrangements.'

What he didn't tell me was that the entrance exams for Alleyn's had already been sat, and that he had to make special arrangements with the headmaster for me to be considered for one of the sought-after assisted places. I don't know what he said, but Mr Grimmett somehow convinced this man who didn't know me to give me special consideration.

As soon as I'd agreed to sit the test, Mr Cook, or Phil, as he now prefers me to call him, spent hours during breaks and lunchtimes tutoring me for the exam. This was not something he had to do; he did it because he wanted to. Both he and Mr Grimmett really wanted to make the lives of their students better, and they knew that, for me, getting into Alleyn's would do this.

The school that was to become my beloved alma mater, Alleyn's, was established in 1882, but has its roots further back, in the College of God's Gift. That school was founded in 1619 by Edward Alleyn, a hedonistic colleague of Shakespeare's who feared so much for the peace of his eternal soul that, in his will, he left a large chunk of his money to fund charitable works. Alleyn's occupies a large site, where the main building, built from beautiful red brick, sits amid lush, green playing fields.

Secondary school is a formative period in most people's lives, and my time at Alleyn's is one that I look back on with immense fondness and gratitude. For me, Alleyn's was a magical place: going there was as exciting as going to Hogwarts was for Harry Potter, and the transformation that it brought to my life was almost as dramatic. It provided me with more than the best education money could buy — it was a place to escape from what was becoming an increasingly miserable home life, and it introduced me to people and ideas that would change me immeasurably. It transformed my notions of the kind of life I could have, and gave me the ability and resources to chase my new dreams aggressively.

It was also the first place where I started to feel that being brown was not going to be a hindrance to my future success or happiness. I rarely heard the word 'Paki' there. I was one of only a handful of non-white students, but the only racism that I encountered was from an old teacher who, when we first met, thought it hilarious to call me 'Sabu the elephant boy'. Yet, apart from this one remark, he treated me no differently from the other children, and indeed took great care of me on one occasion when I severely burned my arm.

The contrast between my school and the housing estate where I lived couldn't have been sharper. Going to Alleyn's every day was like stepping into a parallel universe. I took the 176 bus instead of going through a wardrobe, but the results were the same: I entered a world where things were quite unlike the one I'd left behind.

Perhaps mistakenly, I did my best to keep those two worlds apart. While I never really felt that being brown was an impediment to my fitting in at Alleyn's — I quickly made friends — I found something else to be ashamed of: being poor. The fact that I was probably the poorest kid in the school set me apart far more than the colour of my skin. I was ashamed of my family's poverty, and I tried my best to hide it from my new friends by never inviting them to my home and rarely going out with them in case they wanted to do something that I couldn't afford to. I couldn't believe how lucky I was to be going to such a school but, at the same time, I started to realise that money and social class were perhaps more important than race when it came to determining one's potential success in life.

My background set me apart in another way at Alleyn's. The official religion of the school was Christianity, and it was customary to sing hymns during morning assembly. I still thought of myself as a Muslim, so when asked by a teacher whether I wanted to be excluded from this part of the assembly, I said yes unthinkingly, believing that doing so was somehow expected of me. I was one of only two students in my year who did this. The other was a Jewish boy, and we became good friends through the few minutes we shared at the start of each school day when we were excluded from the rest of the school. I think that both of us felt a bit self-conscious and a little embarrassed as we'd stand in the corridor together while the other students traipsed in past us. The whole thing made me feel very uncomfortable, and after the first two years I made the decision to join the rest of the students for the full assembly, and stood up with everyone else in the hall as the hymns were being sung. I never actually sang along, though — not just because I have an awful singing voice, of which I am embarrassed, but because I felt silly singing songs of worship to a God I didn't believe in. And, I suspect, because I still had some lingering bits of guilt that I was doing something 'against my religion'.

My time at Alleyn's was instrumental in exposing me to different cultural values and beliefs. I began to see that I did not need to be defined by the colour of my skin — the doors of a 'cultural supermarket' were opened for me, and I began shopping there, starting to create an identity of my own choosing.[10] I embraced the fact that I felt different (doesn't every teenager?)

and, in some ways, I set out to make my difference more pro-nounced, perhaps most obviously by dressing in a manner that can only be described as experimentally extravagant. For the first five years of my time at Alleyn's, I had to wear a school uniform, but I grew my hair long, got an earring, and even experimented with nail varnish and eyeliner (it was the 1980s).

Getting my ear pierced was a pivotal moment in my ado-lescence. I had it done at age 13, soon after my mother died. I honestly thought it looked cool, but even so, the main reason I got it done was that I knew it would piss off my father, as well as the other old Bangladeshi men on the estate, because good Muslim boys didn't wear earrings. The earring was my way of telling my dad and the wider community that I wasn't going to be who they wanted me to be.

The evening after I had it done, my father found me watching television with a gold stud in my ear. I was sur-prised by the calmness with which he said, 'You've got your ear pierced.'

I looked him straight in the eye and said, 'Yes, I have,' leaving unspoken the challenge, 'What are you going to do about it?'

He glared at me for a while and then walked away. I smiled in quiet celebration; I had won. It was a crucial moment in our relationship — perhaps the moment when we both acknowledged that he and I were no longer in a traditional father–son relationship, that I was in some ways his equal. A few weeks later, I went as far as wearing a small crucifix in my ear, but this time my father said nothing.

Later, in the sixth form, when we were allowed to wear our own suits, I purchased ones that pushed at the boundaries of what the school would find acceptable — including a salmon-pink suit, and another that, in a stroke of glorious tackiness, had a hood attached to the jacket. I wore embroidered, patterned shirts and my hair in a ponytail. (What was I thinking?) Outside of school, I dressed predominantly in black, and tried for a while to emulate the goth look. I spent hard-earned money from my part-time jobs on ridiculously tight black jeans (for which my family still make fun of me), and a black leather biker's jacket and black suede boots, both with silver zips and buckles all over them. I wore long, dangly earrings in the shape of daggers or snakes, and I sculpted my sideburns so that they were long and pointy.

I must have thought I was being original with all this, wearing different clothes and earrings and hairstyles from those around me. In reality I was a living cliche, one of countless pained teenagers who embrace outlandish clothing and hair as a means of signifying to the world just how different they are. The fact is, I could never make a particularly convincing goth — apart from the fact that I was brown (and surely a true goth should be pale white, like Brandon Lee in *The Crow*), I wasn't really into goth music, instead preferring pop music and soul by the likes of Luther Vandross and Alexander O'Neal. Far from looking cool and sexy, as I might have imagined back then, I suspect I looked like someone who was playing dress-up with stuff that had been thrown out by Michael Jackson, Prince, and The Cure's Robert Smith.

I also did all these things as a way of saying to the world, 'Look, I'm a grown-up, I can choose how I dress.' It was a way of asserting my independence. I wanted to look different from my friends at school and at home because I felt different from all of them. But there were other factors that played a part in my extreme fashion choices, too. If I'm honest, part of me was simply seeking attention. I wouldn't have admitted it at the time, but these things were probably a reflection of my confusion and insecurity about my identity.

While I may look back with embarrassment at the way I used to dress, I'm glad I went through that phase. It showed that I was thinking about who I wanted to be and how I wanted the world to see me. I wanted to be in control of what people thought about me, and I didn't want to be defined by those things that had defined me in the past — my skin colour, my parents' religion, and what sociologists called my 'socioeconomic roots'.

Experimenting with dress is, of course, a common way for young people to assert their identities. While perhaps only a minority go as far as I did, most make conscious decisions from a young age about what to wear. Music and fashion play a large role in helping young people arrive at their identity. But for some, religious belief can be the crucial factor in determining how they identify and present themselves to the world. For example, there were a number of students at my school who identified strongly as Christians, wearing cruci-fixes around their necks and going to lunchtime meetings of the Christian Union. Such clubs still exist in schools around the western world — probably particularly in the United States — bringing together students who feel that their 'love of Jesus Christ' is central to their identity. For example, on the website of the Sandown Christian Union, it states: 'Basically we're all about loving Jesus together, telling everyone who will listen how awesome His saving grace is, and seeking to back up our words with action.'[11] But I suspect that what these clubs actually do is not that different from other forms of youth subcultures in terms of providing their members with a sense of identity.

One of my best friends, now an atheist, was a member and then leader of my school's Christian Union. She has told me that it gave her 'a sense of family and belonging' and that, for her, it was 'a platform for being rebellious at the same time as righteous'. Whereas I had chosen to be non-conformist through the way I dressed, membership of the Christian Union gave her a way of challenging her peers. She wrote this to me in an email:

> I guess (looking back on it now) it was a proxy war — a way of saying 'I'm proud of who I am', 'I'm not afraid of you' — sentiments I would love to have felt in many other contexts, but didn't. I would have loved to be able to feel (and say), 'It doesn't matter that I'm not cool' and 'I am worth as much as any of the rest of you.' I couldn't, but I could say, 'I'm a Christian and I don't care what you think about that.'

My friend's story will probably resonate with many. A large number of people around the world will be going through or will have gone through the same experiences as her, and will seek or will have sought comfort, security, and an identity in embracing the religion of their parents. This is especially true of young people.

It seems to me that, today, an increasing number of teenagers are actively choosing to adopt a distinctly Islamic identity in order to define themselves. Young men grow beards and wear clothing typically worn in Arabic cultures — long-tailed shirts over baggy, thin cotton trousers that swing above the ankles, and a topi, or skullcap, on the head. As far as I know, there is no religious commandment that requires them to dress in this way. However, 'Arab' clothing has come to signify 'Muslim' clothing and, for men in the west, such outfits provide a way to clearly signal to the world that they are Muslim.

Similarly, young women may choose to wear a hijab (which covers the head), niqab (which covers the face, leaving only the eyes visible), or burqa (which covers the face and body, with the eyes visible only through a veil). These items of clothing, perhaps more than the outfits of young Muslim men, seem to many in the west to symbolise not only an overt embracing of Islam, but an explicit rejection of western values. As writer Kenan Malik notes:

> In Britain, and in the West more generally, Muslim women choose to wear the niqab as an affectation of identity. They are

often young, middle class, highly articulate professionals, far removed from the usual stereotype of the cowed, oppressed Muslim woman. So why wear the niqab? To make a statement. 'Look at me, I am different,' they are saying, 'and I want to be seen as different. I have my own values and beliefs and I want to have nothing to do with the values and beliefs of the rest of you.'[12]

Many of the Muslim women I know would claim that it is their choice to wear the hijab or niqab, and that they do so because that is what their faith requires of them, not because it is demanded of them by husbands, fathers, or brothers. Some might agree with the notion that a headscarf or other covering liberates them from 'the intrusive, commodifying, basely sexualising Western gaze'.[13] But I have also heard reports of young Muslim girls feeling pressured by their peers into wearing the hijab, and even of a strange competitiveness among some ('You only wear a hijab, whereas I wear a niqab'). I know at least one young woman who wears a hijab because she has no choice to do otherwise. This is an individual who, at the age of 16, went from taking an active interest in women's fashion to wearing traditional Islamic dress almost overnight. When I asked her why she had undergone such a drastic transformation in her appearance, she replied, 'My brother has become a strict Muslim.'

To me, and to many other people, the niqab and burqa are unnatural forms of clothing, invented to oppress women and keep them 'in their place'. They seem to me a physical representation of some of the least palatable ideas that Muslims can hold based on their beliefs, ideas about the status of women and the nature of human sexuality; to me, they seem to symbolise the attitude that women are inferior to men, and appear to be evidence of a deeply unhealthy attitude towards sex. However, despite my reservations, I would rather live in a society that allowed women to choose to wear these items of clothing than one in which they were forbidden from doing so, or indeed forbidden from wearing whatever they wanted. As long as I am free to hold and express my views, others should be similarly free to exercise choice over their appearance.

As well as clothing, some young Muslims adopt political views which they feel convey their devotion to Islam, identifying themselves with the 'struggles' of their 'brothers and sisters' in places like Palestine and Afghanistan. This is a manifestation of what Gary Younge, in his book *Who Are We — and Should It Matter in the 21st Century?* describes as 'the push for authenticity'. He writes:

> The push for authenticity runs deep in identity politics and corrodes from the inside. At its most powerful and insidious, it creates a form of self-policing whereby everyone assumes that everyone else is meeting an abstract ideal standard apart from them. At its root, it insists that who we are necessarily determines what we do and how we think.[14]

Others put it more bluntly, such as Muslim writer Qanta Ahmed, who states, 'Many first- and second-generation British Muslims shun their ethnic heritage and cultural frameworks in favour of a perverse, exaggerated, narcissistic compassion for worlds of which they will never be part.'[15]

It seems to me that, in some ways, some of the young Muslims in the west who choose to embrace their Islamic identity so strongly may be behaving in a way that is little different from their goth, indie, hip-hop, and even Christian counterparts — they are responding to an innate need to assert an identity. Many grow up out of this behaviour and recognise it for what it is — a search for identity rather than a search for God.

However, not all teenagers have the same degree of choice about these matters. Some are forced by their parents to present themselves to the world in terms of their religion first and foremost. For example, boys from Sikh families are usually made to wear their hair in a *patka*; Hasidic Jews require their adolescent men to keep long sideburns, known as *payot*; and the Amish make their children wear simple clothing in plain colours because they believe that you should not take pride in your appearance. Both men and women from Orthodox Jewish families are required to dress 'modestly', the same idea that makes some Muslim parents demand that their daughters wear head coverings such as the hijab. Many young Jewish and Muslim girls are not free to wear garments that might reveal skin other than that of their face and hands.

And it's not just in dress that young people are told to adhere strictly to the laws of their parents' religion. They can be forbidden from listening to certain kinds of music or, sometimes, even any music; seeing certain kinds of films; going to parties; and, perhaps most sadly, mixing with children from different religious backgrounds. They are deprived, unfairly, of the entitlement to explore who they want to be or the freedom to express who they feel themselves to be. This, the stifling of young people's right to determine their own identity, is perhaps the most unforgivable aspect of all religions.

Our identity is central to how we think of ourselves, and it determines how we interact with others. But 'identity' is a misnomer — none of us has a single identity. Instead, we all have a multitude of identities that we assert in different ways on different occasions. For my part, I am a teacher, a writer, a brother, a Bangladeshi, a British citizen, and an atheist. I'm also a terrible singer, an over-enthusiastic eater, a literary snob, and a vain man approaching middle age concerned about losing my hair and putting on weight. Each of these identities is important to me, but any can take precedence over the others depending on the situation I am in. As Gary Younge writes:

> The decisions as to which [identities] we assert, when we want to assert them and what we want to do with them are ours. But ... [d]ecisions about which ones we prioritise do not take place in a vacuum. They are shaped and sharpened

by crisis. We have a choice about which identities to give the floor to; but at specific moments they may also choose us.[16]

For many Muslims living in the west, the events of 9/11 and the resulting Islamophobia have, understandably, forced them to identify more strongly as Muslims. For me, one of the saddest outcomes of this atrocity is that the actions of a tiny, tiny minority of Islamists have forced a wedge between Muslims and the rest of the world, a wedge that they did not ask for, creating a barrier that only compassion and empathy will break down.

While I empathise with many Muslims and understand why they might choose to assert this aspect of their identity, it is one that I have explicitly rejected. Not just because I don't believe in Allah, but also because I feel that it is my duty to assert my own identity as an atheist. I feel that it is important for people like me to be 'out' because there are not enough such people from a Muslim background who are willing to be open and honest about their lack of belief in God, and this makes it difficult for young people from these communities to be who they want to be. The sad truth is that I am a rare breed — a public 'ex-Muslim' — and one of the reasons I have written this book is to let countless others who keep their lack of faith a secret know that they are not alone. This may sound overdramatic or self-aggrandising but, on the other hand, at least I don't believe I'm one of a special people 'chosen' by God. My delusions are of my own making.

While I will continue to ponder my beliefs, I suspect that I will never go back to Islam, never again call myself a Muslim. I don't doubt that there are still some out there who would call me a 'coconut' because of this. But if what that means is that I have freely made my own choices about who I want to be and how I want to live, then I am proud of the label.

FIVE

GOD IS LOVE

I ONLY RECENTLY admitted to myself that my mother loved my father. For years after her death, I refused to accept this fact. I told myself that, if only she had lived a little longer, I would have rescued her from him; I would have given her a better life.

I know now that this would not have happened — my mother would never have left my father, no matter what he did to her. And the things that he did to her were a large part of the reason why I spent years resenting him. Worse than the fact that he was quick to hit her, worse than making her live in poverty, he made my mother endure act after act of humiliation, including forcing her to sleep with us children while he had sex with his mistress in their marital bed. My mother had to suffer through months of shame while this woman lived in our home. It was a shame with which some of the other Bangladeshi women on the estate could empathise — many of their husbands had second wives back in Bangladesh, a practice that is not uncommon in Islamic countries, where polygamy is sanctioned by Qur'anic law.

Before my father decided that life on the dole made more sense to him than going to work, he was a chef. He'd come home late at night, exhausted from being on his feet all day. More often than not, my mother would stay up, waiting for him to get home and making sure that he had something hot to eat. My father would sit on the sofa with his dinner, and my mother would fill a white plastic tub with hot water and wash his feet, scraping away at his corns and calluses with a pumice stone. It always seemed to me that this was just another of the many duties that she had to perform as a wife. But looking back, I realise that she did it because she wanted to. She didn't just give my father's feet a quick scrub; she took her time, massaging and caressing his feet, enjoying being in his presence after a long day without him. Of course, I never saw it in this way as a child — children are largely innocent of the mechanics of romantic love, and it is only as an adult with romantic longings of my own that I can see just how and why my mother might have loved my father.

Very few of my parents' generation of Bangladeshis would have had a 'love marriage'. Most of them would have been arranged, and love would be something that might or might not have developed at some later point in such a marriage. It was a lucky dip: I have friends whose parents are clearly devoted to each other, while at the same time there are many Bangladeshi couples from that generation who can barely tolerate each other. (Perhaps not so different from non-arranged marriages.) And the tradition continues: even today, a lot of Bangladeshis, including some of my friends, have had their marriages arranged for them.

Wealth and social status are top of the list of things that people look for when planning their children's marriages, and my mother's parents would have been no different. Although Bangladesh does not have the same rigid caste system as India (Islam is more egalitarian in this respect than Hinduism), there is an established social hierarchy that can limit people's options when it comes to marriage. My mother and father were well-matched socially: while my mother's family may have been slightly wealthier, my father's family owned a good deal of farmland and had the additional social status associated with having a high-ranking army officer as their eldest son (he would later die a hero in the war against Pakistan). My father also had good prospects of 'becoming someone', having been educated to secondary level — a rare accomplishment in the community of which we were part.

Arranged marriages often don't take into account other factors that might make two people compatible life-partners, and this can sometimes result in acrimony (just look at what happened to Prince Charles and Lady Diana). Fortunately, my parents got off to a good start. From what I can gather, my mother must have fallen in love with my father pretty quickly. It's not hard to see why: he was a good-looking, charming, intelligent, and ambitious young man. I imagine that she must have been pleased with her parents' choice. My father couldn't have been disappointed with his luck, either — my mother was a beautiful and smart young woman. I suspect that, unlike in some arranged marriages, physical attraction was not a problem for either of them.

Romantic love can have powerful effects on how a person sees the world and, in particular, the person they are 'in love' with. My mother's attitude towards my father — that is, loving him despite his awful treatment of her — was not unique; it is not at all unusual for people who are in love to refuse to see their beloved in a negative light. This is usually more true for newly smitten lovers, who, according to social psychologist Ellen Berscheid, 'often idealise their partner, magnifying their virtues and explaining away their flaws'.[1]

I have been in love. I have experienced both the hell of unreciprocated love and the heaven of being loved back. In one case, for far too brief a time, I lived the very ideal of 'true love' and was happier than I ever imagined I could be. But that's another story. The key is that these experiences of love and loss were perhaps as formative for me as the death of my mother and, in some ways, have caused me as much pain and sorrow.

I once read the sentence 'I tell cows about you' in a book of Magnetic Poetry. I instantly knew what it meant, and I suspect that if you have ever have been in love, you will know, too. It conveys perfectly the state you find yourself in when you've just fallen in love and want to tell the whole world about how wonderful your beloved is. It's sometimes known as 'mentionitis' — the compulsion to drop the name of the person you're besotted with into every conversation, even at the most inappropriate of times. Mentionitis is just one of the symptoms of being in love. And 'symptoms' is precisely the right word to use because, just as the symptoms of a cold are the result of chemical changes in your body following infection by a virus, our behaviour when we are in love can be understood as the results of chemical changes in our brain.

We can look to science to explain some of the more extreme behaviour caused by being in love (although it may offend some romantics to do so). Scientists have identified the changes in brain chemistry that accompany falling in love, and have revealed that there are good physiological reasons for the strange behaviour that those who are smitten sometimes exhibit. Studies involving MRI scans of the brains of 'recently smitten' college students show that 'the experience of romantic attraction activated those pockets of the brain with a high concentration of receptors for dopamine, the chemical messenger closely tied to states of euphoria, craving and addiction'.[2] If you've ever been in love, you'll recognise the feelings that dopamine can bring about — increased energy and wakefulness, decreased appetite, and a greater sense of excitement and enjoyment of life in general, particularly when doing things with, or related to, the new love in your life.

Falling in love and being in love are wonderful experiences that have the power to transform and enrich our lives unlike anything else. Romantic love is more than worthy of all the great works of art, literature, and music it has inspired.

There is only one thing that has rivalled romantic love in inspiring artists, writers, and musicians: belief in God. And the similarities between belief in God and love do not end there. Many psychologists, including Lee Kirkpatrick and Phillip Shaver, believe that 'the psychology of love can teach us something important about religion'. Kirkpatrick and Shaver have carried out research which supports the hypothesis that 'people's beliefs about God or other deities — and especially their conception of having a personal relationship with this God — may be in some sense functionally equivalent to human attachment relationships'.[3]

Some of my best friends have been in love with people I really couldn't stand. However, good manners prevented me from telling them so at the time. If I had decided to tell my friends what I really thought of their girlfriend or boyfriend, it's unlikely that he or she would have thanked me for my wisdom and dumped the offending person. In fact, it's far more likely that it would have been me who was dumped as a friend; telling someone how you really feel about the person they love is a risky thing to do. Even in extreme cases, when we can see that our friends are in love with people who might really hurt them, voicing our concerns would largely be futile because, as the saying 'love is blind' attests, people in love are often, in a very real sense, blind to any faults in the person they are in love with.

You can probably see where I'm going with this. People who identify strongly with a particular religion or hold a strong belief in God often behave in the same way when anyone questions or challenges their beliefs. Philosopher Daniel Dennett says that the 'discomfort or even outrage' that religious people feel when asked to consider the pros and cons of their religion is 'the same reaction one feels when asked for a candid evaluation of one's true love'. Dennett argues that a strong belief in God 'isn't just like falling in love; it is a kind of falling in love'.[4] If we accept this, we can see why otherwise rational people cling to irrational religious beliefs, and why it is often a futile exercise to argue about religion with theists.

The idea that romantic love and religious love are connected is not entirely outlandish. Indeed, many religious people may be proud to declare that they are 'in love' with God. I was startled by an example of this when, as part of my efforts to teach myself Spanish a few years ago, I bought a CD by Mexican singer Marcela Gandera. The album had song titles like 'Supe Que Me Amabas' ('I Knew You Loved Me') and 'Antes De Ti' ('Before You'), each consisting of romantic lyrics along the lines of 'Before you … there was no song in my heart, there was nothing in me.' I initially thought they were cheesy love songs, but as my Spanish improved I worked out that when Marcela was singing 'señor', the Spanish word for 'sir', she wasn't being weirdly polite to her lover: she was using the word to mean 'Lord'. Marcela was singing these love songs to Jesus. It led me to the realisation that the entire genre of Christian rock relies on music and lyrics that I suspect most people would associate with romantic love, not God.

While it may make some people feel awkward to admit that romantic love and religious love can be the same thing, science raises an even more uncomfortable thought. If we accept, as evolutionary psychologists and other scientists encourage us to do, that love is a result of a brain chemistry which has evolved due to the pressures of natural selection, we might find ourselves arguing that belief in God is also a product of human evolution. The evolutionary psychologist Jesse Bering makes a strong case for this idea in his book *The God Instinct*; he argues that our capacity for belief is something that carries 'powerful evolutionary benefits'.[5] Ultimately, this reasoning leads to the conclusion that God may be an illusion, something that the human brain has invented to help us survive — a kind of scientific way of arriving at Voltaire's conclusion that 'If God did not exist, it would be necessary to invent Him.'[6]

There is one other comparison that I want to draw between religion and love. Just as being in love can be a temporary condition, so can belief in God. Just as people fall out of love with other people, they can fall out of love with God; and just as some people look back on former lovers and wonder, *What was I thinking?*, former theists can cringe at the thought of having been a 'believer'. As a teenager, I believed that my first love would be my only love; I could not imagine not being in love with that person. People who believe in God must experience something similar — it must be impossible for them to imagine what it's like to not believe. But just as I got over my first love, lots of people undergo 'deconversion' experiences and leave behind the God they may once have thought was central to their happiness.

I find it fascinating to read about the science and psychology of love, but I must make something clear here — arguing that love is a result of evolution and of brain chemistry does not in anyway diminish the beauty or power of that love. It does not make being in love any less special or important. Science can help us to understand why it is such a powerful emotion and why it plays such an important role in human affairs; but while I am fascinated by what it has to tell us about the nature of love, it has played no part in helping me to deal with the reality of being in love. This is unlike religion, which often seeks to guide, if not to control, love.

My parents, like the parents of most of my Bangladeshi friends, never kissed each other in front of their children. Public displays of affection seem to have been taboo; they rarely touched each other in even the most casual of ways in public. When on the street, the men would walk several feet in front of the women, a sight that is not unusual in Muslim communities even today. This behaviour was at odds with my view of romance as a child: I believed that there could surely be no pleasure sweeter than holding the hand of a beloved while strolling down a street.

But romance wasn't entirely absent from my home life. Like many other Bangladeshi families, we devoured Bollywood movies, which mainly consisted of dashing heroes declaring their love for beautiful heroines through extravagant gestures that involved singing, dancing, and beating up baddies. I suspect that Bollywood movies — and, indeed, most movies about love from all over the world (except perhaps French ones) — are responsible for perpetuating unrealistic expectations of romance. Yet I can't help but feel that they are ultimately less harmful than some of the ideas that a religious upbringing can give people about love and romance. Not to mention sex.

It is impossible not to acknowledge that both Islam and Christianity seem to have an unhealthy preoccupation with sex. As Sam Harris put it in his *Letter to a Christian Nation*: 'Your principal concern seems to be that the Creator of the universe will take offense at something people do while naked. This prudery of yours contributes daily to the surplus of human misery.'[7]

Many people brought up in religious homes grow up with the notion that sex is dirty or sinful. Yet sex is among the most natural things we can experience; it is the very epitome of a 'natural instinct', a desire that is absolutely demanded of us by the fact that we are living creatures. Reproduction is necessary for life, and a desire for sex is what allows nature to ensure that animals like us reproduce. Without it, the human race, like all other animals, could not have evolved in the way that it has. It is paradoxical that we are naturally predisposed to want lots and lots and lots of sex, but a religious upbringing can make people feel that they need to suppress their sexual appetites, leading to psychological suffering and feelings of guilt and shame.

Many of the taboos around sex in the western world have their roots in Christianity. German philosopher Friedrich Nietzsche wrote, 'It was Christianity ... that first made something unclean out of sexuality', and indeed there is plenty of evidence that pre-Christian cultures had a very different, and arguably healthier, attitude towards sex.[8] Much Christian theology seems to treat sex as a necessary evil, the sole purpose of which should be reproduction. This is an idea that probably has its roots in writings of Augustine, a theologian who lived over 1,500 years ago. Augustine is regarded as one of the most important figures in the development of western Christianity. He believed that the male erection, instead of being a perfectly natural response to sexual arousal, was evidence of man's sinful nature — that it was some kind of 'revolt against God' by the male body. Augustine's writings propagated the idea that sex outside of marriage was a sin and should only be permitted for procreation. These were, of course, views that he expressed only once he had fully embraced Christianity, before which he was quite happy to have sex outside of marriage with at least two women.

Augustine is also acknowledged by many scholars as having been responsible for the development of the concept of 'original sin', which is perhaps the most heinous idea at the heart of Christianity. Original sin is a basic tenet of Christian theology which essentially states that all humans are born in sin because Adam and Eve disobeyed God in the Garden of Eden. As usual with these sorts of matters, theologians have different interpretations of exactly what this means, but the common story is that God made Adam, and then made Eve from one of Adam's ribs, and placed them both in a heavenly garden where they could do whatever they liked, except eat an apple from a particular tree. Satan turned up in the form of a snake and 'seduced' Eve into eating the apple, and it is this act that led humanity to fall from paradise and turn into the miserable, sinful creatures we are today. Craig A. James, author of *The Religion Virus*, argues that the concept of original sin 'leads to the conclusion that women are responsible for all the evil in the world' and thus 'Augustine laid down the theological foundation for reviling women' — something that manifests itself today in the Catholic Church's continued refusal to allow women to become priests.[9]

But Christianity is not alone in being fundamentally misogynistic when it comes to sex. Ibn Warraq, the author of *Why I Am Not a Muslim*, writes, 'To call Islam sex-positive is to insult all Muslim women, for sex is seen entirely from the male point of view; women's sexuality is admitted but seen as something to be feared, repressed, and a work of the devil.'[10] The most obvious manifestation of this in Islam is the requirement for women to be covered up, but a more extreme example is the practice of female circumcision (or, to give it its more accurate name, female genital mutilation), which is practised in many Muslim communities and in which the clitoris of young girls is removed with the specific intention of reducing, or even entirely destroying, their ability to enjoy sex.

Islamic theology seems to accept that sex is a natural pleasure that should, in the right circumstances, be indulged in.
There are strict guidelines about it, but there is also an
acknowledgement and even encouragement of the pleasure
that it can provide. Yet Islam's view of sex, it seems to me, is
confused and sexist. On the one hand, men are asked to
'lower their gaze' in the presence of women; on the other
hand, Muslim men are promised all sorts of sexual rewards
after death. Fifteenth-century Qur'anic commentator Al-
Suyuti wrote that in heaven:

> the penis of the Elected never softens. The erection is eter-
> nal; the sensation that you feel each time you make love is
> utterly delicious and out of this world and were you to
> experience it in this world you would faint. Each chosen
> one will marry seventy houris [sometimes translated as
> 'virgins'], besides the women he married on earth, and all
> will have appetising vaginas.[11]

Basically, once they die, there'll be endless sex for those
who want it, as long as they've been Good Muslims here on
Earth. As with so much religion, there is the notion that suffering and going without in the real world will be compensated
for in the afterlife. But if a Muslim misbehaves sexually in this
life — for example, by having premarital sex or by committing
adultery — Islam dictates that he or she may be punished by
stoning or whipping, a sanction that is still carried out in many
Islamic countries today.

The idea that sex is sinful is not common to all religions, nor indeed even to all denominations of Christianity, Judaism, and Islam. Some Jews see sex as a divine gift, and some New Age cults have regarded orgasms as a way of communing with God.[12] But one idea that is common to all of the Abrahamic religions is that sex outside of marriage should be forbidden. This may have been a sensible rule to adhere to in the past, when there were only primitive and ineffective means of contraception. It is easy to see how this rule could have protected women, in particular, as they may have otherwise been left in the position of having to take care of a child without the support of a man, something that would have been very difficult in times when societies were even more patriarchal than they are now. However, like so much in religion, a rule that may have been logical and useful — much like forbidding the eating of pork because it was a frequent transmitter of illness — has been enforced by claiming that it is something required by God. It has been transformed into an issue of morality, when really it was no more than a practical concern.

Today, many people are still brought up to believe that sex before marriage is a sin, and the resulting feelings of guilt and shame may spoil what should otherwise be a joyous experience for them. This is ridiculous in an age where there are reliable means of contraception, such as condoms and the pill, that can hugely reduce the possibility of pregnancy if used properly. There are risks and problems associated with having premarital sex, particularly for young people, but promoting abstinence based on an outdated and sexist religious morality is not the way for society to deal with it. As Andrew Copson, chief executive of the British Humanist Association, says:

> The only way to prevent unwanted pregnancies, the spread of sexually transmitted diseases and unhealthy, unfulfilling relationships is good-quality sex and relationships education, which accepts the reality that young people will have sex, and that what we need to do is help them to do so safely. [13]

In addition, the fact that many people have premarital sex despite their religious leanings suggests that these people don't feel that such sex is immoral in the way that, say, killing someone is immoral. I suspect that forbidding premarital sex is another of those anachronistic rules that mainstream religions will eventually let go of as they try to remain relevant.

It is one of life's tragedies that most of us can't have sex whenever we feel the urge. However, nature has provided us with a way of relieving our sexual urges without the need for a partner, a method that can give us intense physical pleasure and doesn't (usually) harm ourselves or anyone else. Most medical and sex experts would agree that masturbation is a natural and harmless expression of sexuality for both men and women. Masturbation can help to relieve sexual frustration and stress and, in men over a certain age, can even reduce the risk of prostrate cancer.[14] Masturbation can also help us to become better lovers by helping us discover what turns us on. However, once again, religion can turn something that is entirely natural and benign into something that causes guilt, shame, and anxiety, all of which can lead to serious psychological harm.

Of all the major religions in the world, it is perhaps Catholicism that has the most pernicious views of masturbation, and indeed of sex in general. In 1975, Pope Paul VI issued a declaration, 'Persona Humana — Declaration on Certain Questions Concerning Sexual Ethics', condemning masturbation as a 'grave moral disorder'. He wrote:

> masturbation is an intrinsically and seriously disordered act ... the deliberate use of the sexual faculty outside normal conjugal relations essentially contradicts the finality of the faculty. For it lacks the sexual relationship called for by the moral order, namely the relationship which realizes 'the full sense of mutual self-giving and human procreation in the context of true love'. All deliberate exercise of sexuality must be reserved to this regular relationship.[15]

One interpretation of the Catholic stance on masturbation is that doing it even once is enough to send you to hell, provided that you know it's a sin.

It's not just masturbation and extramarital sex about which the Catholic Church has unhealthy views. It insists that sex is intended only for procreation, and so bans the use of most forms of contraception, including the ones that work best: the pill and condoms. One negative consequence of this is, of course, that Catholic families who abide by the Church's rules on contraception can have large numbers of children, even if they do not have the means to support them. But in recent years, an even worse outcome has emerged from this particular rule — the loss of innocent lives through the transmission of HIV.

Right now, over 22 million people are living with HIV in sub-Saharan Africa, and close to two million more are being infected with the virus every year. Over a million people in the region die every year from the AIDS that develops as a result of the virus, and there are more than 12 million children who have been left orphaned by the disease.[16] It is an epidemic that is devastating these countries.

HIV is a sexually transmitted disease, and we know that condoms prevent its transmission. There is no medical debate about this. And yet the Catholic Church and many other Christian groups continue to spread the message in Africa that the use of condoms is immoral, thus preventing millions of their followers from protecting themselves from the risk of HIV. Journalist Tanya Gold is perhaps justified in accusing the Catholic Church of committing a 'holocaust' with its anti-condom stance.[17]

In late 2010, there was some excitement in the media (and, no doubt, among Catholic families) that Pope Benedict XVI had changed his position on the use of condoms. However, it was not much of a shift. This is what he wrote:

There may be a basis in the case of some individuals, as perhaps when a male prostitute uses a condom, where this

can be a first step in the direction of a moralisation, a first
assumption of responsibility, on the way toward recovering
an awareness that not everything is allowed and that one
cannot do whatever one wants.

A male prostitute is a very specific case, hardly a step
towards allowing the use of condoms among the general
population. He wrote later in the same document: 'But it is
not really the way to deal with the evil of HIV infection.'[18]
The Pope and his followers, and millions of Christians of
other denominations, believe that sexual abstinence and fidel-
ity are the answer to the AIDS epidemic. Sadly, they are
mistaken, because while humans are perfectly capable of following a rule that says 'don't use a condom', they are not
capable of not having sex.

My greatest love affair was with an American atheist from a
Christian family. I don't have the words to do justice to how
wonderful an experience it was, but you'll know how much
it means if I say that being with her made me feel loved in a
way that I hadn't since my mother died. At the risk of losing
some readers at this point, I'm going to make reference to a
Coldplay song and say that she 'fixed me'. That's all I'm going
to write on the subject except to add, Reader, I married her.

The point I want to make is that, if I had stuck to being a
Good Muslim, I would never have had what was one of the
most beautiful, rewarding experiences of my life. This is

because Islam, like most religions, does not only concern itself with when and how we can have sex, but who we can have sex with.

Most religions insist that you do not marry someone of a different faith. This is a good way of ensuring the propagation of the religion, but it is something that must have led to millions of broken hearts throughout history. I have more than one friend who, unlike me, did not marry the love of their life because the girl was not of the same religion. There are countless stories throughout history of people from all religious backgrounds who have let religion come in the way of being happy with someone they love. Even today, Hindus, Muslims, Jews, Catholics, and Protestants are disowned by their families and expelled from their communities for falling in love with someone from the 'wrong' religion. Perhaps whoever first said 'love conquers all' should really have qualified that with something like, 'Love conquers all unless your religious beliefs make you feel unable to follow your heart.'

One way around the obstacles of marrying someone from a different faith is for one person to convert to the other's religion. I know of a number of people who have made the pragmatic decision to convert to Islam because that was the only way to be with the person they loved. While in some cases the conversion may be genuine, I imagine that in most circumstances the obvious dishonesty of such 'conversions' is simply easier to live with than it would be to lose face in the community. I know of a white English man who converted to Islam to marry a Bangladeshi woman, but both are now secretly atheists. They keep up the pretence of being Muslim so that the woman can stay on good terms with her family. It saddens me that, even in the 21st century, people like this couple do not feel free to be who they really are.

Agreeing to adopt the religion of your beloved is an uncommon gesture of commitment, but any romantic relationship worthy of the name brings forth at least one occasion when a commitment of sorts is made: the moment when one person tells the other, 'I love you.' Hearing these words for the first time must be one of the highlights of anyone's life. Of course, I mean 'I love you' in the romantic sense, not in the way that your parents might say it to you. When I was a teenager, I was not at all unusual in longing to hear these words. I imagined that if a girl ever said 'I love you' to me, my life would somehow become a better, happier one.

When I did eventually hear those words, during the summer in which I was 17, I was completely taken by surprise. I was working in the catering department at the National Theatre on the South Bank in London. A few of my Bangladeshi friends were also working there, and it was a fun summer, hanging out with each other at work and messing around whenever we got the opportunity. I also made friends with some of the other staff, including one who has remained a lifelong friend. Towards the end of the summer, I started to feel that something had gone awry with our friendship, and wanted to spend some time with this friend to try to fix it. The two of us decided to go for a walk after work one evening, but ended up just a couple of hundred metres away, at one of the most romantic spots in London, overlooking the River Thames. After some casual banter, I raised the issue and asked what was going on — had I done something wrong? He told me that I had done nothing wrong, but something had changed. I asked him what, and that's when he said, 'I love you.'

I was stunned. It was completely unexpected. I had no idea that he was gay, let alone that he was in love with me. I don't remember exactly what else we said to each other, but my response to him was along the lines of the same unbearable response I would get a few months later from the first girl to whom I would make the same declaration: 'I love you, too, but just as a friend.'

Although this friend and I never became lovers, I have always treasured what he said to me. He had fallen in love with me because of our friendship; he knew me really well and loved the person I was. He made me feel something that I have not always felt — that I was worthy of being loved. For this reason, I felt that his declaration of love was beautiful and pure. And yet, many religious people would see it as an ugly abomination because it was a man in romantic love with another man.

The Abrahamic religions are all fundamentally homophobic, and many homophobes today justify their prejudicial views by quoting scripture. In 2009, a gay man in New York was viciously attacked by two men who were disgusted by his homosexuality. A friend of the attackers was interviewed on television, and claimed that the man 'deserved' the beating because he had 'blown a kiss' at these friends — but what was particularly telling about this man's homophobia was that he had a tattoo on his arm reading 'Thou shalt not lie with another male as one does with a woman. It is an abomination. Leviticus 18:22.'[19] Somewhat ironically, Leviticus 19:28 states: 'You shall not make any cuts on your body for the dead or tattoo yourselves: I am the LORD.'[20] Like so many other religious hypocrites, this man quoted the Bible when it suited him and ignored it when he chose to.

Leviticus 20:13 suggests that gay men should be put to death: 'If a man lies with a male as with a woman, both of them shall be put to death for their abominable deed; they have forfeited their lives.'[21] Although few Christians would act on this, it can be used by some to justify hate crimes. For example, in January 2011 an American Christian killed a 70-year-old gay man because 'he read in the Old Testament that gays should be stoned to death'.[22] Worse, in many Islamic countries homosexuality is strictly illegal, and punishment can range from a violent beating to death by stoning.[23] The recent spate of homophobic violence in certain parts of Africa has been fuelled by both Christian and Muslim leaders calling for communities to 'flush out gays'.[24] These religious leaders would no doubt quote scripture to explain their actions. Apologists for the Bible and Qur'an have nowhere to hide on these matters; their holy books are undeniably filled with homophobic ideas, and followers of these religions will always be able to justify their prejudices by claiming that they have God on their side.

When adults hold these kinds of attitudes, it is not surprising that children do, too. I have had students in my science class tell me that homosexuality is unnatural because 'God made Adam and Eve, not Adam and Steve'. This pathetic line of reasoning is not much worse than the arguments that religious adults offer, explaining their homophobia by saying it is 'a deviation, an irregularity, a wound'. At a time when progressive societies around the world are pressing forward with equal rights for homosexuals, the Pope has said that same-sex marriage is one of the 'most insidious and dangerous challenges that today confront the common good'.[25] How can we tell children off if adults are spouting this kind of nonsense?

There is nothing unnatural about homosexuality; some people just happen to be attracted to those of the same sex. The love between a gay or lesbian couple is fundamentally no different from the love between a man and a woman. It is sad and tragic that the Pope, along with priests and imams all over the world, continues to promote the idea that homosexuality is evil, sinful, or somehow against God's will, because in doing so he sanctions the cruel treatment of gay men and women and prevents otherwise good people from questioning homophobia. To revile homosexual love is to revile the love that is central to the experiences of millions of our fellow humans, and this is something that is genuinely immoral.

I have often seen signs outside churches that read: 'For God so loved the world, that he gave his only Son.' It seems like an attempt to make us feel that we owe this God something, the desperate plea of someone who says, 'But you must love me, I've done so much for you.' That's not how real love works. To me, it works when we give freely without expectation of anything in return, and when we care more deeply about the happiness and wellbeing of other people than we do for ourselves.

Love is important. Our experiences of it are often the most defining ones of our lives. And I don't just mean romantic love; I mean all the forms of love we can experience, such as the love of our family and the love of our friends. Love can bring out the best in us and drive us to be the finest, noblest people we can be. Perhaps more than anything else, it is love that can provide meaning in a world that can often seem meaningless.

The Bible and Qur'an are filled with passages that tell of God's or Allah's love for humanity. Indeed, the New Testament, in John 4:8, tells us that God is love. But from what I can tell, this is not true; God is a poor substitute for love. I would not deny that loving God may have psychological benefits for those who really believe, but it is ultimately an unreciprocated love, because a being that does not exist cannot love you back.

SIX

MY FATHER'S SON

LIKE MOST LITTLE BOYS, I loved my mother best — not that my father offered much in the way of competition for my affections. Whereas 'Amma' had been the very model of motherhood, my father seemed to lack all but the most basic of parental instincts. I'm sure I frustrated my mother on many occasions, but I never set out to displease her. It was different with my father — not only did I not care whether he was upset by my actions, but I also actively rebelled against him. Soon after my mother died, my siblings and I started to refer to him as Tom, an acronym for 'the old man', so that we could talk about him in his presence without him knowing (being children, we thought it was clever, but I suspect he knew what we were doing). Even today, we refer to Tom rather than Dad, reflecting the sad truth that we really didn't think of him as a father in any meaningful way.

Yet my father was a remarkable man, something of a local legend in the Bangladeshi community in which I grew up.

He was one of the few Bangladeshis in the neighbourhood who could read and write English (or Bangla, as it happens), and he helped many of our neighbours to fill in their application forms for council housing, social-security benefits, and all of the other things that require copious paperwork and come with being an immigrant. He sat on the board of a charity that set up a hospital in his hometown in Bangladesh and, during the first Gulf War, he held court in our living room, reading newspaper accounts of the war to an audience of the local elders — something of which I was begrudgingly proud. I remember them huddled around him in the living room, drinking tea and listening while my father, in his strongly accented but melodic English, would read the latest reports of events in Iraq, an Islamic country with which they felt a kinship.

My father was charming. You know the kind — the one that other guys want to be like and that girls want to be with. He won people over; they couldn't help liking him. Once, a social worker came around to investigate his treatment of us — we were probably on an 'at risk' list somewhere — but she left the house convinced that he was a model parent. If she had not fallen for his charms, my childhood might have been very different.

If I hadn't been his son, I would have looked up to my dad. From the outside, he was by far the coolest of the Bangladeshi dads on the estate, not least because he dressed better than all the others, wearing stylish suits, shirts, and ties, instead of looking like he'd 'just got off the boat'.

He was tall for a Bangladeshi man (a trait I wish I had inherited) and carried himself with a self-confident swagger; in the late 1970s and early 1980s, he could have passed for a brown version of John Travolta.

Another thing of which I was secretly proud was that he was definitely the toughest Bangladeshi man on the estate. He was the only one who ever dared to stand up to the racist thugs who regularly terrorised the Bangladeshi community. I remember him chasing a couple of skinheads down the road with a big cooking knife in his hand. They had been spraying 'NF' (the acronym of 'National Front') on my uncle's car, and my father was not going to let them get away with it. A few months later, rather amusingly (or perhaps rather scarily), one of my younger brothers, Aslom, used the same knife to chase a couple of boys who had been bullying Shahajahan, who was at the time the youngest in our family. I suppose that made my father a role model in some respects.

While my father's brilliance was obvious to anyone who knew him, so were his flaws. He drank, gambled, womanised, and lived a life filled with self-gratification. He was given to indulging his passions — something that made him unsuited to fatherhood. Yet, ironically, he would have at least ten children; when he died, aged 65, his youngest would be just over a year old.

Like many dads on the estate, my father beat his children. He also bullied me into giving him money that I had earned from my part-time jobs. But my feelings of anger and resentment towards him did not stem so much from his treatment of me as from the way that he had treated my mother — and the way that he effectively deserted my siblings soon after she died. He was far from being grief-stricken upon my mother's death; instead of turning to Allah for comfort, he turned to an illiterate 16-year-old girl from a village in Sylhet, our hometown, in north-west Bangladesh. He had been making the arrangements for the marriage even while my mother lay in a coma. Within weeks of her death, he left us to stay with a relative in east London while he went off to Bangladesh. I remember with embarrassment the moment I saw him packing an entire suitcase with boxes of condoms. At 13, I was old enough to know what they were for, and my father knew that. 'They're for your uncles,' he told me. Which may have been partly true, but I doubted that my uncles were virile enough to get through all those condoms on their own.

He returned a couple of months later with his new wife, who was barely older than me. Even in our community, which turned a blind eye to pretty much everything my father did, there were mutterings — if he had wanted someone to take care of his kids, neighbours commented, he should have married a widow or an older woman. It was very difficult to avoid the conclusion that he had simply picked a beautiful young bride to satisfy his own needs. I heard some of the other men in the community talking about how my father had gone and gotten himself his own Hema Malini (a gorgeous actress from the Bollywood movies we all watched). My father's happiness was short-lived, however, and his actions brought about great unhappiness for everyone concerned.

My father's gambling was also at the heart of much of our misery when we were children — it was the reason we were even poorer than the other Bangladeshi families in the neighbourhood, regularly going without decent food and clothing, and it was the cause of many arguments that my father would have with my mother and then his second wife — arguments that he would ultimately 'win' by beating them.

It was evident to my siblings and me that my father was not a Good Muslim. Apart from the drinking and gambling, which a lot of the other Bangladeshi men on the estate engaged in (albeit more surreptitiously), my father also failed to conform to other demands of Islam. Unlike his drinking and gambling buddies, once he reached 'old age' he did not grow a beard, start wearing Islamic clothing, or become a regular at the local mosque. He rarely fasted during Ramadan, although he'd pretend to do so if we had visitors. He'd even lie to us about it, but we'd see him having a cup of tea or smoking a cigarette in the mornings before we went to school. Every once in a while, usually after he had done something awful — gambled away his week's wages or come home drunk or gotten further into debt with the local moneylender — he would make a big show of praying five times a day. My siblings and I would find it hilarious to see him lay out his rarely used prayer mat, put on a topi, and recite his prayers in a dramatic manner in his effort to let my stepmother know that this time he had really changed. His reformation would last a few entertaining days before he'd revert to his usual ways.

My father didn't try very hard to make us observe Islamic practices and customs that he himself would not. Despite the many things for which I resented him, I am extremely grateful that he didn't force Islam on me too strongly. I think that's because he didn't really think it was that important. Because, deep down (and apparently not very deep down), he just didn't buy it. I suspect that the only reason he made any attempt to make me and my siblings go to the mosque and endure some of the other religious rituals demanded by Islam was to keep up appearances with our neighbours.

I'm inclined to think that keeping up appearances is responsible for much of the religion that lingers in western society. Despite what some atheists might think, I doubt it takes a great deal of intelligence or education to see that many religious customs and beliefs are anachronistic, or to hold the suspicion that the God of the Bible and Qur'an is a human invention. But it's simply easier for many people to pretend that these thoughts never cross their minds, so that the boat of the community in which they reside is never rocked.

I think that my father may have wanted to be a Good Muslim, in much the same way that many other people I know want to be Good Muslims. The problem, as with many other religions, is that being a Good Muslim pretty much takes the fun out of life. No sex outside marriage (hell, Muslims don't even want you to look at a woman), no alcohol, and no bacon sandwiches make for a dull existence. And there is so much fun to be had, especially in the west, where we have the advantages of robust systems of government and freedom of expression. I can't help but think that many of those extremists who rail against 'western decadence' are simply deeply jealous of all the fun everyone else seems to be having. Yes, I'm being facetious, but only a little.

There are many reasons why people believe, or claim to believe, in God. In 1998, Dr Michael Shermer, the founding publisher of *Skeptic* magazine, and Dr Frank Sulloway, a social scientist at MIT, carried out a survey in which they discovered what they called an 'intellectual attribution bias' when people are asked about why they believe in God; that is, 'people consider their own beliefs as being rationally motivated, whereas they see the beliefs of others as being emotionally driven'. These were the five most common answers given to the question 'Why do you believe in God?':

1. The good design/natural beauty/perfection/complexity of the world or universe (28.6 per cent)
2. The experience of God in everyday life (20.6 per cent)
3. Belief in God is comforting, relieving, consoling, and gives meaning and purpose to life (10.3 per cent)
4. The Bible says so (9.8 per cent)
5. Just because/faith/the need to believe in something (8.2 per cent)

These were the six most common answers given to the question 'Why do you think other people believe in God?':

1. Belief in God is comforting, relieving, consoling, and gives meaning and purpose to life (26.3 per cent)
2. Religious people have been raised to believe in God (22.4 per cent)
3. The experience of God in everyday life (16.2 per cent)
4. Just because/faith/the need to believe in something (13.0 per cent)
5. Fear death and the unknown (9.1 per cent)
6. The good design/natural beauty/perfection/ complexity of the world or universe (6.0 per cent)

The same researchers found that that the seven strongest predictors of belief in God are:

1. being raised in a religious manner
2. parents' religiosity
3. lower levels of education
4. being female
5. a large family
6. lack of conflict with parents
7. being younger.[1]

These findings lend support to the idea that the primary reason for most people belonging to a religion is that they have had some sort of religious upbringing or, as some people might call it, childhood religious indoctrination. Organised religion is a cultural construct, transmitted through our culture by our parents and communities. I once pointed out to a group of 15-year-olds that everyone in the class who was a Muslim had Muslim parents, that all the Christians had Christian parents, and the Hindu students' parents were Hindu. I asked them to think about whether, in light of this fact, we could really assert that everyone in the class had come to their own conclusions about what to believe. It was a small example, but the students realised that the principle could be generalised to society at large. It was the first time that many of them had thought about it.

A minority of people claim to have experienced some kind of personal revelation from God; a larger minority grow up to think deeply on these matters, weigh up the evidence, and come to their own conclusions about the existence or non-existence of God. But it is evident that most people who claim to believe in the Abrahamic God do so because they are brainwashed into it from birth. As Sam Harris writes in *The End of Faith*:

> [Y]ou are likely to be the product of a culture that has elevated belief, in the absence of evidence, to the highest place in the hierarchy of human virtues ... every child is instructed that it is, at the very least, an option, if not a sacred duty, to disregard the facts of this world out of deference to the God who lurks in his mother's and father's imaginations.[2]

It seems obvious to me that people who really believe in a god would want their children to believe in the same god, as they would want them to find the same joy in belief. It is likely that they would deliberately set about indoctrinating them. But it also seems to me that, usually, deeply held beliefs and the joy derived from them are not what really motivates people to indoctrinate their children with a belief in God. I would suggest that most people do so almost by accident, without even thinking about it. The overwhelming majority of children are taught that God exists from the minute they can learn anything. They are subjected to elaborate rituals, such as christenings and religious festivals, that reinforce the significance of this thing called God and the importance of belief. In short, they are surrounded by people who act as if God exists, so there is no reason to suspect that God does not exist.

It's only once children start thinking for themselves that belief in God first wavers but, even then, the indoctrination or conditioning they have experienced when they were young makes it difficult for most to develop their own thinking on this issue. Adults present religious stories to children as being 'true' and categorically different from the other stories. As Sam Harris has observed, 'each new generation of children is taught that religious propositions need not be justified in the way that all others must'.[3]

Most children are also brought up with the impression that it is evil not to believe, and that they will be punished — often in horrific ways, such as burning for an eternity in hell — for deviating from the rules and regulations of their parents' religion. Children brought up in one of the Abrahamic religions will be told stories of Satan (*ha-Satan* in Hebrew and *Shaitan* in Islam), a supernatural being who is almost as powerful as God and whose intention is to prevent them from believing in God. Children are told that if they don't believe in God, or if they doubt the truth of their religion, Satan has done his job. Thus, those who start to have doubts about the existence of God are encouraged to think of themselves as morally bad people and, because they don't want their parents, or anyone else, to think of them in that way, they pretend to believe. This pretence is carried on into adulthood, and the whole vicious cycle continues.

I think the idea that it is immoral to not believe in God is perhaps the most insidious one that parents encourage to take root in the minds of young children. It is what makes it so difficult for people to question the existence of God once they have acquired the ability to think and reason for themselves; the nature of humanity is that once we believe something to be true, it can take a lot more than reason or evidence to change our minds. I can't help but think that my being an atheist is at least partly because that my parents did not make enough of an effort to indoctrinate me, and because my contact with the Islamic community of my childhood was more limited than that of my Muslim friends. It seems that my father's failure to set a good example in a religious sense was instrumental in my own 'failure' to become a Good Muslim.

I understand why the concept of a god exists. I understand why humans are compelled to reach for meaning and moral guidance through such an entity, because there have been times in my life where I would have given anything for an external source for these things that we all crave at some time or other. As Dr Justin Barrett, psychologist and author of the book *Why Would Anyone Believe in God?*, says: 'It is easy, it is intuitive, it is natural. It fits our default assumptions about things.'[4] To me, there's no doubt that religion is a fundamental aspect of being human. There are no god-free cultures in history, as far as I know, and plenty of evidence that the idea of a god turned up pretty early in pre-history.

However, I'm not convinced that very many of the 'religious' people I know believe in a god in the explicit sense of the word. Surely if you really believed in an omnipotent, omniscient god — one who insisted that you live in a particular way if you are not to be damned to all kinds of hell for eternity — you would never live in any other way. Or, as the philosopher Daniel Dennett put it, 'You wouldn't masturbate with your mother watching you! How on earth could you masturbate with God watching you? Do you really believe God is watching you? Perhaps not.'[5]

There's pretty strong evidence that our ancestors really believed in supernatural powers and life after death — otherwise, why would they have made sacrifices to the gods of things they could ill afford to sacrifice, or buried their dead with things that would have been of far more use to the living? These people literally put their money where their mouth was when it came to belief. But few people today carry out such practical acts of belief (although when they do, it can have horrific consequences, from Jehovah's Witnesses who refuse blood transfusions when critically ill to members of religious cults who commit mass suicide in the belief that they are going to join God). Suicide bombers are often held up as examples of people who have a firm belief in the truth of their religion, and it seems logical that such people must be absolutely convinced of the existence of God. Yet even among such a seemingly devout group, there is some evidence that they carry out their missions not so much through unfaltering belief in God as through an un-wavering commitment to their fellow conspirators — a kind of submission to an extreme form of peer pressure.[6]

While it would be difficult to prove, I suspect that most people — at least in the west — who profess to 'believe' in God are not true believers, but believers in belief. Such people are convinced that believing in a god, having 'faith', and following a particular religion are Good Things. They want to believe in God, even if they don't really believe. Some of these people eventually convince themselves that they do believe in God and are happier for it, but many maintain a pretence about it for their whole lives, ignoring or actively denying their true feelings about the non-existence of God.

As a child, I was pretty sure most people around me believed in God. However, as I grew up, I became convinced that my father did not. I wonder how many of the people I know today who claim to be religious actually believe in

God, and how many are just believers in belief. I don't think I've met many people who are absolutely sure of the existence of God. The few people I have met who fall into this category have been, frankly, odd. (For example, a Christian who actually shed a few tears for me because I was missing out on the glory of God and would not be going to heaven despite being 'such a good person'.)

It seems to me that, in the 21st century, with our increased levels of knowledge and education, belief in God simply stretches our credulity too much; it is too irrational. But we are conditioned to believe that belief is good by our upbringings and by a culture that, despite itself, continues to give religion an undeserved status as a Good Thing. I suspect that this is one reason why extremists of all faiths hate atheists more deeply than they hate each other — because we don't even believe that belief is important.

My father was one of those millions, if not billions, of people around the world who did not really believe in God, but believed in belief. This was sufficient for him to make us go to the local mosque to learn how to pray and recite suras from the Qur'an. But my siblings and I hated this; it was boring and inane. We made little effort to progress with our Islamic studies. It is telling that, for a bunch of kids who performed way above average at school, none of us managed to learn our prayers or get very far with our reading of the religious texts. I memorised a few suras, and even got as far as being allowed to read the Qur'an, but I never memorised the prayers. On the few occasions in my life that I have had to pray in a mosque (on the festival days of Eid in my youth, and at funerals as an adult), I have muttered nonsense under my breath while imitating the actions of those around me.

When we were young, my siblings and I would do all we could to avoid attending those lessons at the mosque. We would regularly play truant, despite the threat of a beating from our father. One of my brothers would cry with desperation immediately before having to go to these miserable lessons; but, sadly, his tears were never sufficient to move my parents to excuse him from going.

We would also try to escape during the lessons. On one occasion, the imam fell asleep during class and one of my brothers sneakily put the man's watch (the imam had removed it and put it on the floor) forward by half an hour so that, much to the joy of all his students, he ended the lesson prematurely once he was woken up. It was nothing less than a heroic act by my brother — if he had been caught touching the watch, he would have been given a good beating, by both the imam and my father.

I think there was a small part of my father that empathised with the fact that we would rather be out playing than sitting on the uncomfortable floor of the mosque mindlessly reciting suras from the Qur'an. After all, he was, if anything, a dedicated pleasure-seeker. I think that's why he rarely beat us for what would have been considered unacceptable behaviour by other Bangladeshi parents.

The only time I did really hate my father for trying to impose his religion on us was when he had my younger brothers circumcised. He had not had any of us circumcised when we were babies (as would have been the more sensible option), but had left it until we were capable of being terrified of the surgery and fully aware of the prospect of pain. I slept in the same room with my younger brothers, and I nursed them as they recovered. I can't tell you how heartbreaking it was to hear their screams and whimpers every time they moved the wrong way during the night, or when their bandages had to come off for cleaning during the day. I find it hard to understand how anyone could put a child through such unnecessary mutilation and pain for the sake of religion or, as was probably more likely, keeping up religious appearances.

I have a rather embarrassing confession to make here, one that will confirm my status as a kafir: I am not circumcised. On the day the 'surgeon' (I suspect he was just an imam with a scalpel and minimum training) was due at our house, I snuck out early in the morning and didn't go back until late at night, when I could be sure that he had gone. I expected to be thoroughly beaten but, although he was angry, my father didn't lay a finger on me. Perhaps he understood why it would be particularly horrible for a 12-year-old to be circumcised, or perhaps the screams of his other sons that day had affected him. Or perhaps he simply faced up to the truth — that having my foreskin cut off would not have made me any closer to God.

I know lots of people who report being made miserable by their religious upbringing. But even many people who have grown up with unpleasant experiences of religion fail to give up their belief in belief and, rather depressingly, continue to perpetuate religion through indoctrination of their own children. It is belief in belief that prevents so many people I know from breaking free of their professed religions. It is not in the interest of any organised religion to encourage its followers to question or even think about 'belief in belief' because this lesser belief, not the belief in God, is sufficient to ensure the continued survival and propagation of these religions. Actual belief in God or in the other tenets of religion are not themselves necessary.

Societal pressure can lead people to deny their inherent atheism. Religious customs and traditions can be central to the identity of entire communities of people, and individuals who don't believe in God may still want to carry on those traditions and customs because they feel some kind of moral duty to maintain them. So, for example, someone who identifies themselves as Jewish may in fact be an atheist in an intellectual sense, while at the same time insisting on eating only kosher food or only marrying someone who is Jewish. I have heard people claim that some Jews, despite not really believing in God, do these things because if they do not, they feel they will be guilty of 'finishing what Hitler started'.

Suzanne Brink and Nicholas Gibson of the University of Cambridge carried out research into the experiences of people who described themselves as 'ex-Muslims' and found that:

There are cases in which people have ceased to believe in their religion yet continue to pretend to believe in that religion. The reasons behind this decision are generally social in nature. It may be that they are afraid of getting hurt when stating their disbelief openly, or it may be that they do not see enough merit in disclosing their newly found disbelief to justify hurting the people whom they love. They prefer remaining a secret disaffiliate ... Of those making any mention of disaffiliation, around one-third of all narratives included statements to the effect that the authors considered it a necessity to keep their deconversion a secret.[7]

Family and community play an important role in the lives of many people. To be part of a group, we must share values. It may be more important to a person to remain part of a group than to confess his atheism. After all, as friends have pointed out to me, what's the point of rocking the boat, of upsetting your mum? For many non-believers, secrecy and pretence is the only option they feel they have, even as adults, so that they can be good children to their parents. A friend of mine tells me that he 'protects' his mother from his 'true opinions'; I don't blame him for it one bit, as I have no doubt I would have 'protected' my mother in the same way. I can't help but wonder how many people around the world pretend to believe in God for the sake of an easier life.

Belief in belief is a powerful meme. It is one that our society seems to encourage, and one that will only be challenged if more people are willing to come out as atheists, not remain frightened of upsetting the sensibilities of their religious friends, family, and communities to the degree that they remain in hiding.

It seems perverse to say it, but I may have been lucky in having had little in the way of parenting as a teenager. I suspect that, had my mother lived, I would not be so open or outspoken about my atheism; had I thought that it was something she wanted, I would have made more of an effort to be a Good Muslim, or at least kept up more of a pretence of being one. But with my mother dead and a deep lack of respect for my father, I was relieved of the reason why many atheists I know, particularly ex-Muslim ones, continue to pretend to be religious. I no longer had a desire to 'protect' my parents from being upset, or from being 'shamed'. I was freed of the pressure to believe what my parents believed. But this is a pressure that most children have to live with well into adulthood, and it helps explain why ancient religions have managed to survive into the modern world.

Despite his many talents, my father was ultimately an underachiever. His drinking and gambling habits deprived him of the financial resources to invest in business, a common route out of poverty for immigrants. Like so many gamblers, he was looking for the quick win, the easy road to success, instead of working towards a long-term goal that would ultimately have made him happier. Many of his peers went on to own, at least in part, some kind of restaurant or property, and it must have hurt him to see far less intelligent, far less capable men around him leading more visibly successful lives. In the last few years of his life, I felt nothing so much as pity for him because, despite putting his happiness above that of his wives and children, he never seemed to find contentment, and I believe that he died a very bitter, disappointed man. I suspect that he felt this way mostly because he realised that he had squandered not just his time and money, but also the one thing that could perhaps have brought him true happiness — his relationships with his children.

In many ways, I am my father's son. I have his love of and respect for learning; I delight in gambling, playing a regular game of poker with my friends; and I have a fierce temper. But unlike my father, I have put my learning to good use, I gamble in moderation, and I never let my temper take complete control of me. I suspect that I am also like my father in my lack of belief in God. But, unlike him, I don't feel the need to make a secret of this.

SEVEN

LET THERE BE LIGHT

I WAS ONCE kicked out of a physics lesson for blasphemy: I had yelled 'Jesus Christ!' following a spectacular sneeze that left copious quantities of snot over my work. I was in the first year of secondary school, and my wonderful new private education had not yet managed to smooth away some of the rougher edges of my behaviour. My devoutly Christian physics teacher took offence at my outburst and punished me by expelling me from the lesson, and making me write lines stating 'I will not swear in class'. I went on to get top marks in many of the tests she set, but I'm not sure that she ever thought very highly of me. I never could have imagined when I was in that class that, just a couple of years later, physics would become my favourite subject at school, and that I would eventually become a physics teacher myself (albeit one with a distinctly different view of what constitutes swearing).

At the time, I didn't think that there was anything strange about my physics teacher being religious. It never occurred to me that there might be any tension between her role as a science teacher and her personal belief in God. But that was more than 25 years ago, long before 9/11 and the rise of what has been described as New Atheism. Both of these have, in different ways and to different extents, changed the way in which the public think about religion. The events of 9/11 are a defining moment of our era, with repercussions that are still being felt today. There is no single 'truth' about what happened and why, but it will always be thought of as an act of terrorism that was perpetrated by people motivated by religious reasons. It was a stark reminder to many of us in the secular world that religion is not just a personal thing, that it can have implications extending far beyond the private choices of an individual. It was an event that made everybody pay a bit more attention to the role of religion in the world.

It was no coincidence that five years later scientist Richard Dawkins published his book *The God Delusion*, and shortly afterwards made a television series about religion with an even more provocative title: *The Root of All Evil*. Dawkins is regarded by many as one of the world's greatest living intellectuals, and had been most famous, prior to the publication of *The God Delusion*, for his book *The Selfish Gene*, which revolutionised the way we think about the role of genes in biology. *The God Delusion* was a scathing attack on religion that, along with books by Sam Harris, Christopher Hitchens, and Daniel Dennett, was widely credited with popularising New Atheism, a vocal and unapologetically anti-religion movement.[1] While there is some debate as to whether there is genuinely anything 'new' about New Atheism, the movement has certainly helped to make ideas about atheism more widespread and, particularly in the case of Dawkins' book, has helped to spread the idea that religion and science are incompatible.

My own students have grown up in this post-9/11 era, and the questions they ask in class make it evident that, unlike me at their age, some are acutely aware of the tensions between what they learn in science classes and what they know of religion. More than one of my students has asked me if I believe in God, to which I usually reply simply, 'No, I don't.' On some occasions, I have responded to this question by asking, 'What do you think?', to which the student invariably replies something along the lines of, 'You're probably an atheist because you're a scientist.'

While this may seem a reasonable conclusion to draw from the fact that I am a science teacher, it need not have been the correct one. Indeed, I have worked alongside science teachers and scientists who hold strong religious beliefs. To be honest, I'm not sure that science had that much to do with my becoming an atheist, as I am certain that I was a non-believer long before I was a 'scientist'. I suspect that it is the other way around — that I am intrinsically a non-theist, someone who is not satisfied with answers along the lines of 'because of God', is what eventually made me gravitate towards science.

I wasn't always a science geek. I know that it would make a better story to tell you that as a child I had an inclination for exploring the natural world, that I spent my childhood scouring beaches for fossils and building my own particle accelerator in the garage while my parents looked on, bemused but proud. But the truth is, I don't remember doing any science until I got to secondary school. And even then, I found it boring, irrelevant, and frustrating. In the first couple of years at secondary school, I found science difficult, and I'm not sure that it made that much sense to me. My science education suffered from the same problems that turn so many people off science at that age — it was presented as a collection of facts and figures, something done by old white men in lab coats. Sure, I enjoyed burning stuff in chemistry, but I found biology, with all its labelling of diagrams and memorising of names, boring. And physics was just plain hard.

In the early days of secondary school, I had vague notions of wanting to be a lawyer, probably as a result of watching *L.A. Law* on television and reading *To Kill a Mockingbird*, but I certainly didn't want to be a scientist. It was two teachers, Mr Clark and Mr York, who opened up the world of science for me — my journey into geekdom began in their classrooms. Both were gifted teachers whose enthusiasm for their subjects was relentless and infectious. They taught me that science was not just a collection of facts and figures, but a way of thinking; they didn't present me with 'truths' about the world, but told me that they were teaching me about a working model. Each helped me to understand that science wasn't about certainty and rigid facts, but rather a process that made use of deduction, logic, rationality, observation, and experimentation to draw what are ultimately tentative conclusions, leaving the way open for better explanations or theories. It was in their classes that I began to appreciate science and what I think is at the heart of its appeal to people like me: tremendous explanatory power. Science offers us a uniquely successful way of understanding the world and our place in it; it can provide intellectual thrills like nothing else; and it is, possibly, the greatest of humanity's cultural achievements.

Perhaps most importantly, these two teachers taught me that science was a continuing human endeavour, one to which I could conceivably contribute one day. I came to realise that I wanted to be a scientist when I grew up, and left school with a yearbook description that included this now-embarrassing hyperbole: 'Watch out … because this boy is going to find out if God really does play dice.'

I love my friend Jonathan Hassid for writing those words. Not only had he managed to get a reference to Einstein's stance on quantum mechanics into the school yearbook, but he had perfectly encapsulated the youthful optimism and arrogance that we shared as teenagers. Yet I can't look at my yearbook today without a tinge of sadness because things, as is so often the case for many of us, didn't quite turn out as planned.

To cut a long story short, I had a miserable time at university, and ended my time there disillusioned with the world of physics and pretty much everything else. I had gone from being at a school where the teachers had nurtured and encouraged my passion for science to being just another nameless face in a university where the 'teachers' were mostly scientists who seemed to see their teaching duties as a chore that kept them from their real jobs as researchers. As well as dealing with problems at home, I was ill prepared for the drastic change from being a student at high school to being one at university; this accounts, to some extent, for my fall from being a star student to one who barely scraped by. However, the fault was not all mine — looking back on my university lecturers now that I am a teacher myself, I can see that many of them, while perhaps brilliant scientists, didn't have the first clue about teaching, or any inclination to improve their pedagogical skills.

By the time I finished university, I had long given up any dreams of becoming a scientist, and didn't have a clue what to do with my life. My results were far from first class, as I might have hoped for when I was 18, and this excluded me from applying for jobs with any of the banks and corporations that came looking for the 'best and brightest' at university recruitment fairs. I felt as if I had somehow managed to ruin everything that Alleyn's had done for me, and couldn't believe that I had made such a mess of my life.

Yet the seeds of my redemption were to be planted that summer at Camp Homeward Bound, a program for homeless and disadvantaged children from New York, run by the Coalition for the Homeless.[2] I'd wanted to get as far away from my life as possible that summer, and had applied for a job at the camp through one of those organisations that arrange holiday jobs for students. Within hours of arriving at the camp, the director said to me, 'I see you have a physics degree — great, you can teach science.' It wasn't a request, it was an order, and from a no-nonsense man I would quickly come to like and respect. Luckily, another counsellor, known as 'Brother Bear' (the guy was huge), one of the few people at camp actually qualified to teach, took me under his wing and showed me how to plan a lesson. Within a few days, I was standing in front of a bunch of children in a wooden shack in the middle of a forest, teaching my first science lesson. I don't remember exactly what it was about — it was something simple and fun, involving magnets, or soap bubbles — but I do remember that the first time I stood up in front of a group of children as their 'teacher', it immediately felt right, like putting on a new item of clothing that fit perfectly.

During the months I spent at the camp, I felt the malaise that had been enveloping my life gradually lift. The problems of the children forced my own into sharp perspective and, after experiencing a steep learning curve, I spent a long and happy summer being 'Aladdin', a camp counsellor responsible for children aged four to six (some of the counsellors for that age group were named for Disney characters). For the first time in ages, I felt able to be the person I liked to be, the person I missed being — positive and enthusiastic about life.

A year or so later, I enrolled in a teacher-training course and, soon afterwards, found myself teaching science to children aged 11 to 18. It was back in the classroom that my love affair with physics was rekindled, and it has never faltered since. Trying to teach physics has given me the deeper understanding of it that I had hoped to gain at university and has made up for the disappointment that I felt about my time there. After three years of teaching, with my self-confidence restored, I left to try my hand at other things and wandered through a variety of jobs, from working in politics to being a television producer. But after seven or so years away from the class-room, I realised that teaching had been, by far, the most rewarding and satisfying job I had ever had. People (especially other teachers) sometimes ask me why I left the 'glamorous' world of television to go back to teaching. The honest answer is that I have never felt so good about myself as I do when I am teaching. For me, being a teacher satisfies a yearning that many of us have: to be doing something useful in the world. At the risk of sounding cheesy, I teach because 'Mr Shaha' really is the best part of me, the man I want to be.

Teaching has reinforced several of my beliefs about the value of science for young people. Despite many people's experiences to the contrary, science in schools is not just about teaching facts and figures — or, at least, it shouldn't be. It should be about teaching the way in which humans have arrived at answers to questions ranging from how life re-produces itself to how the stars shine. If science teachers like me are doing their jobs properly, science lessons should equip students with skills in critical thinking, the most important of which is, perhaps, to seek evidence for claims about 'truth'. If we've succeeded in teaching these skills, it is inevitable that some of our religious students will ask, 'What is the proof for the existence of a god?' and it's inevitable that some of these students will not be happy with the stock religious answers to this question.

I have been continually surprised by the number of students I meet who have been brought up to believe that the holy book of their particular religion contains the literal truth about the origins of life and the universe. From what I can gather, most of these students approach their science lessons in a rather pragmatic way, accepting that they are required to study the subject until they're at least 15 or 16, and simply get on with learning what they need to know in order to pass their exams. However, I have also encountered some students who genuinely seem to resent having to study material that they believe is 'against' their religion. I once had an 11-year-old student, new to the school, say to me, 'Is it true that you teach evolution in this school?'

I replied, 'Yes, but not in your lessons this year.'

She responded, 'Well, I won't be coming to those lessons. It's against my religion to believe we're descended from monkeys.'

I've had similar conversations with students who believe that teaching about the Big Bang is an attempt to undermine their religious beliefs. More than one has told me, 'You teach us this stuff because you don't want us to believe in God.'

It is not surprising that young people can often be left confused by the apparently contradictory claims of science and religion. Many children are brought up with religious accounts of the world that they believe to be true, since the ideas are presented by figures that are authoritative to them, usually their parents. They then encounter other figures of authority, such as their science teachers, who tell them that the world works in a very different way, and they are expected to regard these ideas as being true, too. This extract from an essay by an American college student shows the dilemma for religious students:

> I grew up with the impression that science and religion were incompatible. Maybe it was because I went to Catholic school, and my religion teacher thought I was trying to be sarcastic when I asked things like, 'If the pope is infallible, why did he say that Galileo was wrong about the sun being the center of the universe?'. When she answered, 'Because the pope didn't know any better', I said, 'Isn't he supposed to know better if he's the pope?', and the teacher told me to stop asking dumb questions and said we'd get into it later (which of course we never did). So out of fear of flunking fifth grade religion AND science, I adopted the policy that what was taught in Science class applied only to science, and ditto for Religion.[3]

It is perhaps reassuring for such students to know that, throughout history, scientists have been confounded by the same dilemma that occupies the minds of children and adults from religious backgrounds. Several geniuses of the past, such as Galileo Galilei and Isaac Newton, are often put forward as examples of scientists who were also religious. Some of these people may or may not have been 'true' believers — it is difficult to tell, as they lived in periods or societies in which it would not have been acceptable to be openly atheist. Other scientists, however, were clearly genuine believers — for example, Georges Lemaître, who was a priest as well as an astronomer, and is credited as being the first person to propose what has become known as the Big Bang theory. Even today, there are a number of prominent scientists who are openly and devoutly religious, including Francis Collins, director of the US National Institutes of Health, and the evolutionary geneticist Francisco J. Ayala, who spent some time as a monk.

Ayala, a recipient of the Templeton Prize for his 'exceptional contribution to affirming life's spiritual dimension', is one of a minority of contemporary scientists who believe that science and religion 'cannot be in contradiction because [they] concern different matters'.[4] His views have been compared to those of the late Stephen Jay Gould, a palaeontologist and evolutionary biologist. Gould wrote that we should think of science and religion as 'non-overlapping magisteria' (NOMA):

> No such conflict should exist because each subject has a legitimate magisterium, or domain of teaching authority — and these magisteria do not overlap ... The net of science covers the empirical universe: what is it made of (fact) and why does it work this way (theory). The net of religion extends over questions of moral meaning and value. These two magisteria do not overlap, nor do they encompass all

inquiry (consider, for starters, the magisterium of art and the meaning of beauty).'[5]

Gould was clearly an intellectual giant who made a huge contribution to science and, through his many popular-science books, to the public understanding of it. However, I can't help but feel that his idea of NOMA was a desperate attempt at diplomacy rather than an intellectually sound position. Perhaps sadly, Gould's version of religion is far removed from the version that most people would recognise. The problem with NOMA is that, as a quick google of the word 'creationism' will reveal, religions do make statements about the world, despite Gould's insistence that this be left to science. It is disingenuous of theologians and others to claim otherwise, particularly when it comes to how religion is presented to young people. As Richard Dawkins has written:

> [I]t is completely unrealistic to claim ... that religion keeps itself away from science's turf, restricting itself to morals and values. A universe with a supernatural presence would be a fundamentally and qualitatively different kind of universe from one without. The difference is, inescapably, a scientific difference. Religions make existence claims, and this means scientific claims.[6]

I understand the urge that drove Gould to put forward his idea of non-overlapping magisteria. The conflict between science and religion can make us feel uncomfortable, particularly when it involves people we know, respect, and love. People take offence when their religious beliefs are challenged. I also understand why some atheists feel frustrated by the beliefs of others, and think that they have to 'correct' them. But, in doing so, they can come across as condescending, patronising, and aggressive. It's not always accidental — several prominent atheists and sceptics have been accused of deliberately behaving like, well, 'dicks', as one atheist blogger put it.[7] There has been a backlash against this kind of behaviour — not just from believers, but also from within atheist circles. While I don't condone the behaviour of 'dick atheists', I can empathise with their frustrations. I'd like to think I'm not one, but I'm not prepared, as I think Gould did, to compromise my intellectual integrity to avoid causing offence. And I will not tell students lies about the world just because it might be what their religious parents would like me to do.

What is it about science that is so troubling to many of those who hold religious beliefs? Inevitably, the most obvious area where religion and science come into conflict is in how they answer the 'big' questions: how the universe and life came into existence.

You might think that I can get away without too much of this sort of conflict in my lessons because I teach physics, and it is biology teachers, the ones who teach the theory of evolution, who have to deal with the awkward situation of presenting something as fact when it appears to contradict the religious beliefs of some of their students. But, as a physics teacher, it's my job to make sure that students appreciate that we have good reasons to believe that the universe is about 13.7 billion years old and that it is filled with thousands of billions of stars. It is my job to teach that the Earth was formed about 4.5 billion years ago from the remnants of an exploded star, and that we, too, are made up of atoms that came from that dead star. It is my job to teach that scientists think that everything — literally everything — came from a tiny point that exploded, creating time and space as it did so. More importantly, it's my job to explain to them why we think this, and admit that we don't yet fully understand how or why this happened. It's my job to make it clear that science is not certain about these things, that scientists are constantly trying to improve our understanding of the world and are open to the idea that they may be wrong, that science is not infallible. However, admitting that science might be wrong about some things is a long, long way from saying any religion might be right.

One of the things that appeals to me about science is that, unlike religion, science is not dogmatic; it does not say, 'This is the way things are, and it can be no other way.' Instead, it says something like, 'Based on the evidence we have so far, this is how things probably are. If clear and solid evidence is discovered that shows this is not how things are, we will need to change our minds.' Science's qualifiers can seem rather weak in comparison to religion's absolutes. But it is this very 'weakness', this refusal to give absolutes, that allows science to progress, and to come up with increasingly better ways of describing the world. However, despite my careful explanations of why scientists think that the Big Bang theory is a good rationale of how the universe came to be, and the caveat that there is a possibility the Big Bang theory is wrong, I have still encountered students who are upset or offended by the suggestion that they should be 'forced to learn this rubbish'.

These same students find the theory of evolution by natural selection even harder to accept. I find this troubling, because there's just as much evidence — if not more — that it is correct. As well as fossils that clearly show the process of evolution in extinct species, we can now compare the genetic sequences of living organisms, thanks to modern scientific techniques. But perhaps the most direct evidence for Darwin's theory is that we can actually see bacteria and viruses evolve under the pressures of natural selection in relatively short periods of time.

Personally, I think that evolution is so troubling to some religious people, and causes them to respond to it as if it is an affront to their human dignity, because they do not fully understand it. This lack of understanding may stem from their lack of engagement with it. When religious people respond to the idea of evolution by declaring flatly, reflexively, that 'we're not descended from monkeys', they have not quite grasped the finer details of the theory because, although it tells us that we share a common ancestor with monkeys, it does not tell us that we are descended from them.

Darwin's theory has been described by philosopher Daniel Dennett as the 'single best idea anyone has ever had'[8] and, given that it allows us to explain so much about the nature of life, no school-science education should be considered complete if it does not include teaching of these basic ideas about how life on Earth evolved. In fact, the explanatory power of this theory is so huge that many scientists would agree with the late evolutionary biologist Theodosius Dobzhansky, who wrote an essay titled 'Nothing in Biology Makes Sense Except in the Light of Evolution'.[9] Interestingly, Dobzhansky was also a religious scientist: he was a member of the Russian Orthodox Church.

Creationists reject Darwin's explanation of the origin and development of life, and instead insist that the version of events described in the Bible is the factual truth. If we are to think in biological terms, it is this belief that defines them as a species: while there may be some differences between individual creationists about precisely what they believe, they all believe that God created humans in the shape and form we exist in today. And creationism is not confined to Christians — many Muslims and Orthodox Jews are also creationists, as they essentially share the same creation story.

Creationists will often say 'evolution is just a theory', meaning that evolution is no more than a guess or a hunch about how life works. When they claim this, they assert that the issue of how life on Earth came about is somehow still open to serious questioning, even though the overwhelming majority of scientists do not think that this is the case.

But these people are taking advantage of an unfortunately widespread ignorance about the way in which the word 'theory' is actually used in science. It arises from the fact that science, like all disciplines, uses language in a very precise way, with narrower meanings than everyday usage allows. For example, the word 'power' in physics only ever means 'the rate at which something converts energy', a meaning that has very little to do with the definition of 'power' that allows us to say that Barack Obama is a powerful man. A scientific theory is one that:

- puts forward a comprehensive explanation for some thing we observe in nature
- provides strong evidence for that explanation
- provides the means with which to make predictions about the aspect of the world it explains, which we can then test by observation.

Among the first great theories of science were those put forward by Isaac Newton, which are known collectively as Newtonian mechanics. His three laws of motion and the law of universal gravitation successfully explained everything from why an apple falls from a tree to why the planets have elliptical orbits around the sun. Newtonian mechanics allowed scientists to make predictions about the natural world, which were then found to be true by observation. Most famously, it was used to predict the existence of the planet Neptune before anyone had seen it. Newtonian mechanics cannot explain or predict all possible situations in nature — for example, it breaks down when dealing with incredibly small objects, such as electrons; or incredibly massive objects, such as black holes; or things that are moving at close to the speed of light. Yet the theories of quantum mechanics, special relativity, and general relativity can explain and predict what happens in these circumstances. This doesn't mean that Newton's theory was ever 'just' a theory; it simply illustrates that scientists are always working to find better ways to understand how nature works.

Like Newtonian mechanics and, indeed, Einstein's theories of relativity, the theory of evolution has been tested, and scientists have found that it successfully predicts the behaviour of living organisms and systems. However, scientists are also open to the idea that the theory of evolution may need to be modified to deal with things that we don't yet know about or understand fully. In short, it takes a lot of work before a scientific hypothesis about how the world works is considered a theory; only science that has passed rigorous testing and met all the requirements outlined above is given the status of a 'theory'. So to describe something in science as a theory is not the cheap insult that creationists might think it is.

Because they view evolution as 'just a theory', many creationists are uncomfortable with the fact that their children are taught about it at school. In parts of the western world, creationists have tried to ban the teaching of evolution and, when that has failed, insisted that students are taught creationism alongside evolution. To aid this bid, creationists have presented the creation story as their own 'scientific' theory:

intelligent design. This is the idea that 'certain features of the universe and of living things are best explained by an intelligent cause, not an undirected process such as natural selection'.[10] The intelligent-design movement has failed to convince the majority of the scientific community to take its ideas seriously because, unlike the theory of evolution by natural selection, it does not put forward a comprehensive explanation for observations in nature, it does not have any convincing evidence to support it, and it has not made any predictions that have been successfully tested. In short, it is not a scientific theory. In order to be considered a scientific theory, intelligent design would need, for example, to tell us who or what is doing the 'designing', and explain the mechanisms by which that entity then creates its finished designs.

Not all devout Christians or Muslims are creationists. The Catholic Church accepts that evolution by natural selection is the process by which life on Earth developed and, like the Church, most Christians would probably agree with a view known as theistic evolution — that is, the view that there is a God who created the universe and life, and also created the process of evolution by natural selection as a mechanism by which His work could be carried out. But there is a vocal enough minority to cause concern, not just through their relentless campaigning against the teaching of evolution, but also through their intimidation of other religious individuals who do not share their views. One example of such intimidation was reported in Britain's *Independent*: several British Muslims threatened an imam, physics lecturer Dr

Usama Hasan, with death after he claimed that Islam was compatible with Darwin's theory of evolution.[11]

Of course, the more literal a person gets about religious ideas, the more likely he or she is to feel conflicted with what science tells us about the nature of the universe. A case that illustrates this perfectly is the Catholic Church's notion that when bread and wine are blessed as part of a communion service, they literally turn into the flesh and blood of Jesus. There is no evidence that this happens, and there is no way, within our current scientific understanding of the world, that this could happen. Anyone with even a basic acceptance of the scientific model of the world will understand that such transubstantiation simply cannot take place, and it is stretching our credulity to ask us to believe that such a thing occurs. Yet the Catholic Church continues to reinforce this myth.

In 2008, Webster Cook, a student at the University of Central Florida, received death threats from Catholics when, instead of eating the Eucharist (the blessed wafer), he walked out of the church with it. Father Miguel Gonzalez, a priest connected with the diocese, described what Cook had done as a 'mortal sin' — that is, a sin that is punishable by an eternity in hell. He said, 'It is hurtful. Imagine if they kidnapped somebody and you made a plea for that individual to please return that loved one to the family. If anything were to qualify as a hate crime, to us this seems like this might be it.'[12] The reactions to this incident might seem quite extreme to anyone who is not a devout Catholic, even if you believe that we should respect other people's beliefs, but this case shows just how powerful religious beliefs can be.

The Catholic Church's demands that its followers accept on faith that transubstantiation occurs, despite there being no evidence of it, shows, perhaps more than anything else, the gulf between science and religion. Science is an evidence-based approach to acquiring knowledge that is open to being proved wrong, whereas religions frequently claim to have absolute, unquestionable, untestable truths about the universe that humans must simply accept. Science absolutely demands that we question its findings; religion prospers when we do not.

I realise that I am at risk of painting a picture of scientists as supremely rational beings who have the perfect approach to knowledge, so I'll pause here to say that there are many scientists and science teachers who are as unthinking and uncritical in their approach to science as some theists are towards their religion. But science does not demand that we believe its findings; instead, it presents evidence and argues its case.

As a teacher, the issue that concerns me is that, although many theologians may argue that questioning religious beliefs is the best way to arrive at the 'truth', many people's religious upbringing discourages them from asking too many probing questions about what they are supposed to believe. It would be disingenuous for anyone to claim that any religion genuinely encourages critical thought in children; far too often, children's questions about religion are met with answers like 'because God made it that way' or 'because it says so in the Bible'. This is reinforced by the fact that belief without questioning is seen as a virtue in some, if not all, religions.

Take, for example, the Christian story of 'Doubting Thomas', one of Jesus' disciples who refused to believe that Jesus had risen from the dead, and demanded proof. Thomas eventually finds himself in the same room as Jesus and is offered the chance to look at his wounds, upon which he concludes that Jesus has indeed come back from the dead. Jesus then says to him: 'Blessed are they who have not seen, and yet have believed.'[13] This tells children that believing without seeing is somehow superior to seeing and believing, that accepting the truth of something is better than asking for evidence. Now, my interpretation of this is open to question, and it could be argued that this is really a story about how life is more difficult for those who have doubt in their faith and that Jesus will eventually show them proof, but my feeling is that this story, at least when it is presented to children, is an attempt to stifle critical thinking and to make an attribute of unquestioning faith.

Some religious people might argue that I believe in science the same way that they believe in God — that I have 'faith' in science. But I can, at least in principle, test the claims made by science in a way that we cannot do for religion. For example, in my physics lessons I teach that all objects accelerate towards the ground at the same rate, regardless of their mass. I then get my students to find evidence for this claim by designing and carrying out their own experiments — they do not have to take my word for it, or the word of any other authority figure. And when theists make the argument that science asks us to believe in things we cannot see, such as atoms and electrons, I point out that there are differences between believing in atoms and believing in God: we have theories about what electrons should do if they do exist, and when we test those theories we find that the real world behaves as if our theories are true. For example, modern tele-communications would not work if what science tells us about electrons were not true in some sense. But if we apply such tests to the existence of God, the results come back negative — there is no evidence that any of our ideas about God are, in any meaningful sense, 'true'.

Of course, we do not usually go out and test every single scientific claim we encounter (it would be impractical) and so, in that sense, you could argue that scientists and science teachers have 'faith' in science, but it is certainly not the same kind of faith that is demanded of people who believe in God.

To believe something is to hold a view about its truth. Stating 'I believe that nothing can travel faster than the speed of light in a vacuum' is, to me, the same as saying, 'It is true that nothing can travel faster than the speed of light in a vacuum.' So if someone says, 'I believe God exists', to me they must mean, 'It is true that God exists.' Religion requires individuals to accept certain things as true without evidence. In some cases, such as creationism, religions demand belief in something even in the face of overwhelming evidence to the contrary. In this way, if not in many others, belief in science is far, far removed from belief in God.

In a time before science, God was a reasonable explanation for things that happened in the world — from why the sun came up every day to why people died from disease. Before science, religious explanations were all we had. Priests made predictions, such as that if a child or a virgin were sacrificed, the gods would ensure a good harvest for the tribe. In that sense, any conflict between religion and science stems from the fact that science and religion both have their roots in the same human instinct — the instinct that you can see in any toddler who has just learned to speak, and endlessly asks, 'Why?' As Robert Buckman puts it, 'Religion began as the personification of the because as a spirit or god or animus that held the key to the universal whys. If humans had never wondered Why? there would never have been any gods.'[14]

But, time and again, science has proved to be an entirely more useful method for explaining things and predicting the future than religion. Science makes predictions that can be tested and, unlike religion, scientific predictions work. Science simply offers more-satisfying answers, including an answer to the question, which is not asked often enough by religious people, 'How do you know that?'

I have a lingering disappointment that I never became a 'proper' scientist — that is, someone who added to the body of scientific knowledge in some small way. But I have at least some consolation in having become a science teacher. If my colleagues and I do our jobs properly, our students should go away with a story about the history of life and the universe that I think is far richer, far grander, and far more detailed than that presented in any religious text. More importantly, they should go away with an understanding of how and why this story has come about. If we do a really good job, some of our students might even go away knowing that they can become co-authors of this story by becoming scientists themselves.

I'm not suggesting that science teachers should seek to convert children away from the religions they have been brought up with, or that they should tell them that God doesn't exist. However, a proper scientific education should equip young people to arrive at their own decisions about what to believe, and ensure that, if they do conclude there is a God, He doesn't stop them from fully appreciating the truth and beauty of scientific knowledge.

In the end, clinging to a literal interpretation of the Bible or the Qur'an deprives people of appreciating the glory of scientific understanding. There is no need to jettison belief in God if it gives you comfort, security, or a sense of belonging to a community, but there may be a need to reframe your thinking about how God created the universe. According to the book of Genesis, God said, 'Let there be light.' I can't help but feel that a good God would want that light to be the illumination of education and science.

EIGHT

KAFIR

I HAD A horrible dream, while writing this book, that my brother Aslom was in hospital and about to die. I was the only one at his bedside. We both knew that he had only minutes left to live, and I wanted to tell him not to worry, that I would see him again soon. I almost started to say this, but I knew that my brother would know I was lying. Instead, I hugged him and told him I loved him.

I suspect that this dream was prompted by my writing this book. At a time when I was nearing the end of the process, this nightmare was my subconscious reminding me that there is a cost to giving up God and that, for some people, religious belief has some powerful things to recommend it — not least the comfort it can provide in those situations, such as the death of a loved one, when nothing else can. But the dream was also reassuring me that, in writing this book, I have declared that it is impossible for me to ever tell a lie that is repeated all over the world, often in the belief that it is one from which more good than harm results: the lie that a god and an afterlife exist.

My dream was almost the exact opposite of a crucial scene in *The Invention of Lying*, a 'high-concept' film in which the main character, played by Ricky Gervais, is the sole person who can lie in a world where everyone else can only tell the truth. It starts off as a romantic comedy, but (spoiler alert) takes a surprising turn — one that, unusually, was not hinted at in the trailers I saw — when Gervais's character, in a moving scene at his mother's deathbed, tells her the lie that becomes central to the film's plot. As you may have guessed, the lie is that when she dies, instead of entering a 'world of eternal nothingness', she will go to a heavenly paradise where she'll be reunited with those she loved. In other words, Gervais's character invents the idea of heaven, and since he lives in a world where the idea of a lie is unknown to everyone else, he is quickly elevated to the status of a messiah — able, he tells others, to talk to a 'man in the sky'. The film explores the consequences of this idea before returning to the romantic plot with which it started.

Ricky Gervais is one of a rare breed in Hollywood: an outspoken atheist. With this film, which he co-wrote, he accomplished an astonishing thing: getting millions of people in America, the most religious country in the west, to pay to watch a movie that contained, undisguised, the message that God is a lie.[1] John Mulderig, in a review of the film for the *Catholic News Service*, described it as 'an all-out, sneering assault on the foundations of religious faith such as has seldom if ever been seen in a mainstream film, despicably belittling core Judeo-Christian beliefs'.[2] In an interview about the film, Gervais said, 'It's not meant to be propaganda and it's not me getting stuff off my chest'; however, in a piece for *The Wall Street Journal* written close to a year after *The Invention of Lying* had screened in cinemas, he described how he had left behind his Christian upbringing to become an atheist, and touched again on the idea of God as a lie. He wrote that in order to live an 'honest' life, 'you need the truth ... the truth, however shocking or uncomfortable, in the end leads to liberation and dignity.'[3]

This got me thinking. It's easy to bandy the word 'truth' about in everyday conversation, but things get a bit more difficult when we try to pin down exactly what we mean by it, and why it's so important. In their book *Why Truth Matters*, Ophelia Benson and Jeremy Stangroom write:

> It could be said that everything that is interesting about what it is to be human takes place in this small space: the space between the world as it is in itself, and human understanding of it. The space, that is to say the difference, between true facts, reality, truth, what is Out There, on the one hand, and what we human beings make of that reality, on the other. [4]

It's evident that we humans have an urge, a drive, a desire to know 'how things are'. Perhaps it's a result of how our brains evolved, something that developed to ensure our survival

— for if we can make sense of the world, we can survive all it has to throw at us. It is an instinct that has served us well, allowing us to be successful as a species — spreading across virtually the entire globe, overcoming the adversity of the natural world, and adapting our environment to suit our needs. But this instinct has its drawbacks: it leads us to see patterns where there are none, to accept supernatural explanations for things when there is no need to do so, and to believe things that are simply not true.

What does it mean for something to be true? I'm certain it's true that my mother is dead. No amount of my wishing otherwise can alter that. But I have often indulged in fantasies that the situation is different: that my mother is alive and well in some kind of afterlife or alternative realm; that I am actually still 13 years old and my mother is in hospital, and I am simply dreaming that I am a 37-year-old man writing about his dead mother. These are the kinds of philosophical speculations that can make the mind squirm, and that young people can be delighted and disturbed by when they first consider them. Most of us, however, conclude pretty quickly that such philosophising is largely pointless because we accept that we live in a 'real' world and that there are indeed truths about the world — that is, statements that relate to the world as it actually is. Despite the views of a few solipsists, the majority of us have an overwhelming feeling that we can know meaningful things about the world, things that philosophers, scientists, theologians, and the rest of us are all, in our various ways, on a quest to find out.

If I'm not already, I'm about to get out of my depth as a philosopher here, but let me have a go at explaining how I see things. From my perspective, there is no reason why we should be able to know how the world really is. There is no reason to believe that humans could ever come up with a definitive answer to questions such as, 'What is the world really like?' or 'Where did the universe come from?' Just because we can ask a question does not mean there is a meaningful answer to it — I can ask, 'Do unicorns dream?' but that doesn't mean the question has an answer. If it does, it is likely to be an answer that a human has invented, much like the question 'What does God want me to do?'

Truth often depends on perspective. For example, when my brother Shalim was ill, he believed that he was a crime-fighting superhero being hunted down by comic-book villains. This was clearly untrue to everybody around him, but as far as he was concerned, it was we who could not see the truth. While we all hold beliefs that we have arrived at in different ways, depending on myriad factors, life does not afford us all equal opportunities, and our view of what constitutes the 'truth' will be limited by our circumstances. I have no doubt that my beliefs about the world, for example, would be different if I had not had the particular experiences I've had, and it does not take much imagination to see that I might hold very different beliefs today if my parents had not moved to the United Kingdom; if my mother had not died when I was so young; if I had not gone to Alleyn's; if I had not read the books I have; if I had not known and loved and been loved by the particular individuals in my life. I think I've been lucky that my experiences while growing up have, to an extent, freed me from the shackles of superstition and religion.

I've said this before, but it's worth restating: the acquisition of belief in God is a process that many people have little choice in. It begins when they are too young to question the ideas they are presented with, and is reinforced as they grow up by the fact that, even in the 21st century, even in the developed nations of the world, religious belief permeates our cultural lives to such an extent that not believing in God is still regarded as unusual. As Bertrand Russell put it in 'Why I Am Not a Christian', 'What really moves people to believe in God is not any intellectual argument at all. Most people believe in God because they have been taught from early infancy to do it.'[5]

Let me share an incident that was instrumental in prompting me to write this book: an argument with a trainee teacher. The woman in question — let's call her Susan — was studying to become a religious studies teacher. Over some sandwiches at lunchtime, while chatting with Susan and some colleagues, I mentioned that I thought my science lessons were causing some of my students to re-evaluate their religious beliefs, and perhaps leading them to question what their parents had told them about God. Susan, a devout Christian, was very upset by this. 'You can't do that!' she exclaimed. When I asked what it was I couldn't do, she insisted that it was wrong for children to question their parents; that children should follow their parents' beliefs. I replied that the single most important thing we could do, as teachers, was to teach our students how to think for themselves. If that meant they questioned those in authority, including their parents, so be it. I would like to continue this story by telling you how Susan and I then had a deep discussion about the role of teachers, the nature of knowledge, and the value of a good education. Sadly, the conversation ended with Susan storming off after stating, 'You scientists think you know everything, but you don't!' It wasn't the first time I've had a conversation end in this way, and I suspect that it won't be the last.

I don't for a second think that I know everything. In fact, like most good scientists and science teachers, I'm more than aware that I know very little. But, as a teacher, I am in the privileged position of being able to share what I know with hundreds of young people every year. And here's the thing: whatever Susan and others like her might think, it's not because of teachers like me that children will want to question their parents or even, 'God forbid', their teachers. It's just what children do, unless we adults stamp it out of them by refusing to give them answers, by lying to them, or by threatening them with punishment if they question us — all things that religions require their adult followers to do.

I sincerely believe that, for billions of people around the world, superstition and religion are shackles, things that prevent them from being all they can be. Sadly, there are millions, if not billions, of children around the world who are, by an accident of their birth, destined to grow up without ever having the choice to try living without God. Religion will be the main source of 'knowledge' for these children, and they will remain ignorant, through no fault of their own, of the richness of other ideas out there — scientific ideas in particular. Perhaps even more sadly, there are a lot of adults who might have the same doubts, the same lack of devout belief in a deity, but are prevented from openly rejecting the religion they are born into because of local laws and customs. It would be easy to think that this lack of freedom is something that only affects those living in places like the Middle East or Pakistan, but the reality is that even in the United States, the land of the free and home of the brave, people can be made to feel that they have no choice but to follow the religion of their parents and their community.

When I think of this, I cannot help but believe that, just as many individuals outgrow religion, the human race as a whole needs to outgrow religion. At least, it needs to outgrow the primitive, anachronistic form of religion that still dominates so many people's lives. Some, like Susan, might argue that I am just as bad as religious believers in this desire, that I just want everyone to think what I think. But there is a crucial difference: I want people to genuinely decide for themselves, to make informed decisions, and if having the freedom to do that means that they come to different conclusions about what they believe, then, unless their beliefs hurt other people, I will not condemn them for it. All people, and especially all children, should have the right and the information to be able to work out the 'truth' or otherwise of religion for themselves.

There are some truths that we do not want to face. Sometimes, they are truths about ourselves — perhaps we are not the person we would like to think of ourselves as; we are a little bit uglier, meaner, and stupider than we want to admit. These truths are like objects in our peripheral vision: we can feel that they're there, and could see them if we turned to look, but mostly we ignore them. But just because we deny or reject something does not make it untrue.

It seems to me that the non-existence of the God of the Bible, the Qur'an, and the Torah is one such a truth. Most of us, as we grow up, feel and sense this, but choose to ignore it because it makes us feel uncomfortable. Yet the uncomfortable nature of a truth is not a sufficiently good reason to deny it.

In her book *The Case for God*, Karen Armstrong writes, 'I am concerned that many people are concerned about the nature of religious truth', but it is no wonder that we are confused when Armstrong tells us that 'Jewish, Christian and Muslim theologians have insisted for centuries that God does not exist and that there is "nothing" out there; in making these assertions, their aim was not to deny the reality of God but to safeguard God's transcendence.'[6] She also writes, 'The truths of religion are accessible only when you are prepared to get rid of the selfishness, greed and self-preoccupation that, perhaps inevitably, are engrained in our thoughts and behaviour but are also the source of so much of our pain' and, 'Like art, the truths of religion require the disciplined cultivation of a different mode of consciousness.'[7] I know that Armstrong is knowledgeable about the history of religious belief, but I cannot help but feel that she uses the word 'truth' in a way that does not correspond to most other people's use of it — that is, she does not use the word to mean a statement about the way the world actually is. I have never met a religious person who would insist that God does not exist, and I suspect that any such person would simply, like Armstrong and many other theologians, be playing games with language instead of taking an honest approach to dealing with the questions that we all have about God.

Being an atheist means telling the truth about the non-existence of God. It also means giving up the benefits of religion — from 'knowing' that there is a life after death to the certainty of purpose that comes from believing that God has a plan for each of us, not to mention the sense of belonging to a community with those who hold the same beliefs. It can be hard to fill the gaps left behind when relinquishing these things, and it is perhaps not a challenge for which all of us are equipped.

There are other difficulties in being an atheist, too. Some religious people seem to be offended by the very notion, finding it much easier to relate to someone who believes in a different god than to someone who does not believe in any god. Being openly atheist means that some religious people will automatically see you as someone who thinks they are wrong; in other words, being openly atheist is inherently provocative to some theists. I've had unpleasant encounters with individuals who would have happily beaten me to a pulp for my views. Friendships and relationships have been tested, sometimes to breaking point. And you never know who's going to take offence: a lot of my friends and acquaintances are scientists or hold science degrees but, even for them, religion or lack of it is not a straightforward matter.

Yet while belief in God can often — dare I say usually — be unthinking, I would suggest that it is difficult, if not impossible, for those who have been raised with religion to become atheists unthinkingly. To become an atheist, most people have to actively reject the ideas that were planted in their heads when they were young. Whereas many people who believe in God do so simply because they remain in the default position, like a pre-programmed electronic gadget whose owner has not changed the factory settings, atheists raised with religion do not. In fact, a 2010 study carried out by the Pew Research Centre's Forum on Religion and Public Life found that people who described themselves as atheists or agnostics were better informed about religion than those who believed in God.[8] When this was reported in the *Los Angeles Times*, the article included a quote from Reverend Adam Hamilton: 'I think that what happens for many Christians is, they accept their particular faith, they accept it to be true and they stop examining it.'[9] I think he's right — people of religious persuasions often do not examine, or even question, their beliefs, whereas the examination and questioning of our beliefs is precisely the process that led people like me to become atheists.

Having said that, I hope it's clear that, despite my lack of belief in God, I'm not someone who thinks religious and superstitious people are simply ignorant or stupid. I understand why religion exists, and why some people need it. I understand, in principle, why otherwise intelligent people believe in God. And I understand why some people want to belong to a religion, even if they don't really believe in God. Life is difficult, and the world can be an unpleasant place. The idea of God, heaven, angels, and so on can provide a mechanism for dealing with a reality that is short on happiness. Just as religion can provide some people with answers to the question of how the world is, it gives some people a sense of meaning, solace, and happiness — and who am I to cast judgement on that? In fact, in some ways I think my life would be easier if I believed in God, if I believed in an afterlife, and if I believed that there was a divine plan for me. But I cannot help but believe that meaning and purpose are concepts that we define for ourselves.

The fact is that when people tell you they 'feel' that there must be more than this material reality we inhabit, that's all it is: a feeling. All we can have is a *sense* of meaning and a *sense* of purpose, because there is no divine plan. The God I grew up with is an anachronistic figure who had nothing to offer me. Karen Armstrong might argue that 'God is experienced in the scarcely perceptible timbre of a tiny breeze in the paradox of a voiced silence', but for me this is theological mumbo-jumbo, and 'imaginary friend' comes a lot closer to describing the concept of God with which I think most people are familiar.[10]

It is possible that the appeal of religion might grow stronger for me as I get older and closer to the time when I or, even worse, one of my loved ones, is likely to die. But, right now, it doesn't feel like I have, or had, a real choice about it. As I write this, it feels to me that the truth of the non-existence of God was always there in my life: it was evident in the contradictory stories of God I heard as a child, in the hypocrisy of my father and most of the other adults I knew, and in the absence of any supernatural intervention in the awful things that happen in the world. For me, staring right at the truth of God's non-existence has been a liberating experience — like scratching an itch that had been bothering me and making it go away, leaving behind soft, unmarked skin.

Today, as a result of the formative experiences I have had, I am lucky to have a life filled with the love of my siblings and friends, a love that I cannot imagine could be bettered by a supernatural being. I have meaning in my life through my relationships with the people I know and through my work, and I see the 'point' of my life as being to live it as well as I can, and to contribute positively to the society in which I live. In many ways, accepting there is no God to provide meaning and purpose to our lives can, I believe, force us to create meaningful purposes ourselves.

God is an idea. We live in a world in which we are bombarded with ideas, and people are seeking to infiltrate our minds and create beliefs; we are immersed in a constant war of ideas. People are continually trying to make us believe what they want us to, from mundane things such as that Coca-Cola is the best tasting cola drink or that Nikes are the only sneakers worth wearing, to more important things such as that universal health-care should be paid for by our taxes. These beliefs are what drive our society and, as some people have commented, it may be that, just as our physical bodies are in a way vehicles for the transmission and survival of our genes, our minds may be seen as vehicles for the transmission and survival of ideas, or 'memes'.

God may be the most powerful idea that humans have ever had, but it need not be one that lingers eternally. It has brought comfort and hope to billions, but it is an idea that is easy to exploit for mischief — or worse, evil. If the idea of God were one that invariably made us better human beings — more loving, more caring, and more sharing — perhaps you could argue that it is a belief worth having. But this is not the version of God that I was brought up with, nor is it the idea of God with which billions of others are brought up. And yet humanity clings to this idea. It is time to modify or abandon the idea of God and, along with this, redefine the concept of religion.

Religion is a central influence in the lives of the majority of people in the world, and it is likely to remain so. It is testament to the power of the major world religions that their basic ideas have not changed for centuries. These religions have an inbuilt resistance to change. But that doesn't mean they can't or won't change. I don't think God will ever not be part of human culture. But I have every hope that, with better education, greater freedoms, and the same rights for everybody, humanity may eventually adopt a different take on religion.

I think that atheists can and will play a bigger part in shaping how humans, all over the world, and in all different cultures, think and feel about the needs that religion currently addresses for most people. Perhaps, in the future, societies will rise above the fundamentally divisive nature of contemporary religion and re-invent it to better encompass our scientific knowledge of ourselves, the universe, and morality; perhaps we will shift closer to the idea of religion as a philosophy, a way to provide those who need it with guidance on how to lead better, happier lives without requiring them to think that those who do not believe the same are in some way inferior or deserving of hostility and contempt. As Ophelia Benson and Jeremy Stangroom write, 'Some people do prefer to live in a thought-world where priests and mullahs claim to decide what is true ... Others prefer — genuinely prefer, not merely think they're supposed to — to try to figure out what really is true, as opposed to what might be, or appears to be, or should be.'[11] It will be a huge failure of the human race if we do not evolve better, more relevant, more just ways of living our lives based on our own collective knowledge and wisdom, without having to resort to claims of authority from some supposedly supernatural entity.

This book has been my account of why I don't believe in God. While I have touched upon some of the philosophical arguments for the non-existence of such a deity, I have by no means given an exhaustive account of them. To be honest, I don't think I have much, if anything, to add to these arguments — at least, nothing that you couldn't find in a hundred other books, or simply by googling 'arguments for and against the existence of God'. Philosopher Rebecca Newberger Goldstein, for example, has written a novel that includes, as a non-fiction appendix, 36 arguments for the existence of God and refutations for each of them, and her list is far more erudite than any I could have written. Yet one of the points her book makes is, I think, ultimately the same one that I want to stress here: arguments are not really what drive people to hold or abandon their belief in God. As Newberger Goldstein has said, 'Arguments alone can't capture all that is at stake for people when they argue about issues of reason and faith.'[12] I imagine that very few people have heard either side of any of the classic arguments about the existence of God — the cosmological argument, the ontological argument, the argument from design, the argument from miracles, and so on — and suddenly realised that they were wrong. It's hard enough getting people to admit they were wrong about much smaller issues. I think that, for most of us, a belief in God does not arise or desist because of intellectual arguments. Instead, gaining belief and losing belief are processes, often driven by how we feel rather than what we think, and in which reason plays a smaller role than might be expected or hoped for.

I am not the first ex-Muslim to write about leaving behind the religion of my childhood. There is a book called *Why I Am Not a Muslim*, the title a play on Bertrand Russell's famous 1927 essay, 'Why I Am Not a Christian', by an author who writes under the pseudonym of Ibn Warraq. It provides a detailed critique of Islam and the Qur'an, laying out the author's intellectual reasons for rejecting both. In the acknowledgements, Warraq writes, 'I am not a scholar or a specialist', but his book is far more scholarly than mine and contains far more specialist knowledge. Yet when he writes 'there is hardly an image or thought that I can claim to be my own creation', I can understand and admire his humility because, throughout the writing of this book, I have been weighed down by the knowledge that what I am mostly doing is regurgitating ideas that far greater minds have already expressed with far greater eloquence.[13]

And yet I have written this book because, while I am deeply indebted to Russell, Warraq, Grayling, Dennett, and numerous other great intellects, none of them were remotely responsible for my rejection of religion. And while their work continues to be widely read and distributed, I cannot help but feel that the world needs to hear more personal stories from a wider range of people about why we should, and how we can, live our lives without religion.

While it may be good for the societies we live in to be tolerant about people's views and beliefs, there is no need to accept them as true. If we do so, we demean the concept of truth by reducing what it means to something that is determined by a misguided desire to agree with our fellow humans. While we may want to live peacefully side by side with people who hold religious beliefs, we should not have to say that the God of Abraham is real, that Jesus rose from the dead, or that the Qur'an is the literal word of God in order to do so.

The central tenet of Christianity, the 'truth' at the heart of it, is that Jesus, the son of God, died for our sins. In order to be Christian, you must accept that this happened. According to an even remotely strict interpretation of the Christian doctrine, unless you accept the literal truth of this story, unless you accept Jesus Christ as your 'saviour', you will not go to heaven and spend eternity with God. A question that immediately springs to mind is, 'What if you are born somewhere where you simply might never hear about Jesus?' This is a difficult one for Christians, and is perhaps the reason why, instead of questioning their religion, people throughout history have felt compelled to become evangelists and missionaries, travelling all over the world to spread the 'good news' of Jesus' birth, death, and resurrection.

I have something in common with those missionaries and evangelists. And not just with the Christian ones, but with religious proselytisers of all stripes. I feel that it is deeply unfair that some people may never experience the joy of knowing that they can lead a perfectly happy life, full of meaning and purpose, without God. So, despite my best efforts to be reasonable, empathetic, and understanding about religion, I cannot end this book without this simple statement: I believe that the world would be a better place if there were more atheists, if a greater proportion of the world rejected religion and embraced the view that we humans can make a better, fairer, happier world without God.

I may be mistaken about a lot of things, my arguments may be flawed, and my knowledge on some topics may even be inadequate. But, as I hope I have made clear, this is simply my story of my path to atheism, and yours will be different. If you've noticed the occasional bouts of confusion, contradictions, flawed logic, or misinterpreted ideas, well, they're there because I am a flawed individual, confused and contradictory. I put these shortcomings forward unashamedly, because my final thought is this: none of us is perfectly rational, none of us is in possession of all the possible facts, and none of us is free of beliefs based on irrational foundations. I've laid bare my beliefs because a young atheist's handbook should guide the reader to do one thing: to examine your beliefs and be honest with yourself about why you believe what you do. And if, upon doing this, you come to the same conclusion as me, at least you'll know you are not alone.

As a child, I was taught to say '*La Ilaha Illallahu Muhammadur Rasulullah*' on countless occasions, both at home and in the mosque. I uttered those words mindlessly, not knowing until I was older that they meant 'There is no god but Allah, and Muhammad is the messenger of Allah.' It is a declaration of belief that I was made to recite when I knew no better. Now that I do know better, here's my declaration of unbelief: I am a kafir, an infidel, an apostate. I do not believe in God. I do not believe in God. I do not believe in God. I want to write that sentence millions of times over, once for every person in the world who is not free to write it or say it for themselves. If you are free to say it, join me and sing it, scream it, shout it.

EPILOGUE

IF YOU'VE GOT this far, I want to thank you for reading my book. But I probably owe you a small apology for the somewhat misleading title — after all, it's not strictly a 'handbook'. I hope that, if you've understood anything about me from what I've written, you'll appreciate why I couldn't be the author of anything that had pretensions of being an authoritative text on these matters. Any attempt at writing a 'handbook', in the strictest sense of the word, would have undermined my central argument — that all people, both old and young, need the freedom and opportunity to discover how they want to live their lives for themselves, not have it dictated to them by authority figures of supposedly divine origin or otherwise.

My hope when I set out to write this book was that it would be read, in particular, by those new to the ideas in it, and leave them with the urge to go and find out more. For me, the role of a true teacher is not merely to tell others about the world, but to nurture in them the desire, and equip them with the skills, to go out and learn about it for themselves.

So, why call it a 'handbook' at all? Technically, a handbook is a reference or instruction book providing information on how to do things, or facts about a particular subject. However, as the word indicates, it's also intended as a book that you might turn to for support. Is is presumptuous to use the term in the title of my book? Perhaps. But I regularly see people on the bus or the tube reading worn-out Bibles or other religious texts, and I suspect that, in most cases, they are not reading those books for the first time but using them as a way to stay connected to their faith, or perhaps for comfort in difficult times. There is no such book for those of us who have no faith, although I am sure that many atheists and free-thinkers have their own favourite books that they might use in this way. My hope, and it is an audacious one, is that this book becomes some kind of handbook for at least a few of its readers.

Throughout this book, I have quoted the work of other, superior writers and thinkers, so it should come as no surprise that I wish to include one final quote from a book that is much beloved by many, *The Once and Future King* by T.H. White:

> You may grow old and trembling in your anatomies, you may lie awake at night listening to the disorder of your veins, you may miss your only love, you may see the world about you devastated by evil lunatics, or know your honour trampled in the sewers of baser minds. There is only one

thing for it then — to learn. Learn why the world wags and what wags it. That is the only thing which the mind can never exhaust, never alienate, never be tortured by, never fear or distrust, and never dream of regretting. Learning is the thing for you. Look what a lot of things there are to learn.[1]

I have learned much in writing this book. I hope that you have learned something in reading it, and that this knowledge will benefit you as you continue with your own story.

NOTES

Introduction: Bringing Home the Bacon

1 'Great Facts on Pork', *Islam — The Modern Religion*,
www.themodernreligion.com/misc/hh/pork.html.

2 There are even some groups that promote the consumption of pork.
See for example the website *Jews for Bacon*: www.jews4bacon.com.

Chapter 1: The Day God Died

1 Buckman, Robert, *Can We Be Good Without God?: biology, behavior, and the need to believe*, Prometheus Books, New York, 2002, p. 27.

2 Crick, Francis, *The Astonishing Hypothesis: the scientific search for the soul*, Scribner, New York, 1995, p. 34.

3 Feynman, Richard, 'The Value of Science', address to the National Academy of Sciences, Autumn 1955.

4 Malik, Kenan, 'In Defence of Human Agency', paper presented to the Engelsberg seminar on Consciousness, Genetics, and Society, 14–16 June 2002.

5 Eric Draven (played by Brandon Lee) utters this line to Darla (played by Anna Levine). See Proyas, Alex (dir.), *The Crow*, 1994.

Chapter 2: Being Good

1 Martin Luther King's plagiarism is widely known. See for example 'Boston U. Panel Finds Plagiarism by Dr King', *The New York Times*, 11 October 1991. Biographer Jad Adams wrote of Gandhi's sexual repressions in *Gandhi: Naked Ambition* (2010). The quotation features in an edited extract, 'The Thrill of the Chaste: the truth about

Gandhi's sex life', *The Independent*, 7 April 2010.

2   Hitchens, Christopher, *Hell's Angel*, BBC, 1994.

3   Dostoevsky, Fyodor, *The Brothers Karamanov*, 1888, Farrar, Straus, and Giroux, New York, 1990, trans. Pevear, Richard and Volokhonsky, Larissa. For an example of the paraphrased version, see de Waal, Frans, *Does Evolution Explain Human Nature?*, John Templeton Foundation, 2007.

4   Epicurus is commonly cited as the author of this quote, although its origin is not certain.

5   Depeche Mode, 'Blasphemous Rumours', *Some Great Reward*, 1984.

6   Grandin, Temple, 'Discussion of Research That Shows That Kosher or Halal Slaughter Without Stunning Causes Pain', *Temple Grandin*, February 2010.

7   See for example Deuteronomy 22:20–21 in the New International Version of the Bible.

8   General Assembly of the United Nations, Universal Declaration of Human Rights, article 1, 1948.

9   John 14:6 in the New International Version of the Bible.

10 Malik quoted in Williams, Andrew Zak, 'Faith No More', *New Statesman*, 25 July 2011.

11 See for example Pinker, Steven, 'The Moral Instinct', *The New York Times*, 13 January 2008; de Waal, Frans, 'Morals Without God?', *The New York Times*, 17 October 2010; and Hauser, Marc D., *Moral Minds: how nature designed our universal sense of right and wrong*, Ecco, New York, 2006.

12 de Waal, Frans, 'Morals Without God', *The Huffington Post*, 10 October 2009.

Chapter 3: Escape to Narnia

1   Doctorow, Cory, 'Among Others: extraordinary, magic story of science fiction as a toolkit for taking apart the world', *Boing Boing*, 18 January 2011.

2   The findings of the Early Childhood Longitudinal Study are summarised in Levitt, Steven D. and Dubner, Stephen J., *Freakonomics: a rogue economist explores the hidden side of everything*, Allen Lane, London, 2005, p. 163.

3 George Sayer wrote about C.S. Lewis in his biography *Jack: a life of C.S. Lewis* (1994). The quotation features in an edited extract, 'Jack: a life of C.S. Lewis', *Christian Broadcasting Network*, 2010.

4 For example, Richard Dawkins has said: 'We are all atheists about most of the gods that societies have ever believed in. Some of us just go one god further.' See *The Root of All Evil*, UK Channel 4, 2006.

5 Armstrong, Karen, *A History of God*, Vintage, London, 1999, p. 4.

6 ibid., p. 5.

7 Hsu, Jeremy, 'The Secrets of Storytelling: why we love a good yarn', *Scientific American*, 18 September 2008.

8 Tomkins, Stephen, 'How Biblical Liberalism Took Root', *The Guardian*, 21 February 2011.

9 Paine, Thomas, *The Age of Reason; Being an Investigation of True and Fabulous Theology*, part 1, Barrois, Paris, 1794.

10 Sura 2:282 states: '… get two witnesses, out of your own men, and if there are not two men, then a man and two women, such as ye choose, for witnesses, so that if one of them errs, the other can remind her.' Sura 4:11 states: 'Allah (thus) directs you as regards your Children's (Inheritance): to the male, a portion equal to that of two females: if only daughters, two or more, their share is two-thirds of the inheritance; if only one, her share is a half.' See 'Translations of the Qur'an', *Centre for Muslim–Jewish Engagement*, http://cmje. org. For more on Pakistan's Hudood Ordinance, which places prohibitive burdens of proof on female rape victims, see Wilkinson, Isambard, 'Musharraf Faces Bitter Clash over Rape Law Reforms', *The Telegraph*, 25 August 2006.

11 Sura 2:222 states: 'They ask thee concerning women's courses. Say: They are a hurt and a pollution: So keep away from women in their courses, and do not approach them until they are clean.' See 'Translations of the Qur'an', *Centre for Muslim–Jewish Engagement*, http://cmje.org. Leviticus 15:19–30 suggests that a menstruating woman is unclean, as is all she sits upon and touches. For example, Leviticus 15:19, King James Bible, states: 'And if a woman have an issue, and her issue in her flesh be blood, she shall be put apart seven days: and whosoever toucheth her shall be unclean until the even.'

12 Tatchell, Peter, '200 Years of Church Homophobia', *Peter Tatchell*, 2000.

13 Moses is said to have received the Ten Commandments from God in Exodus 20:17 and tells his followers to kill in Exodus 32:27, King James Bible.

Chapter 4: Coconut

1 'Australia: ignorant bigot organises "ban the burqa" day', *Islamophobia Today*, 17 July 2011; Bryan Fischer and Gary Bauer quoted in Conason, Joe, 'Coalition of Fear: Tea Party, the religious right, and Islamophobia', *Salon*, 20 September 2010; see the English Defence League Facebook page, www.facebook.com/pages/English-Defence-League-EDL/194026250652928?sk=info.

2 'The EDL is a Human Rights Organisation', English Defence League, press release, 28 July 2011.

3 Conway, Gordon, 'Islamophobia: a challenge for us all', report of the Runnymede Trust, 1997.

4 Allen, Christopher, 'Islamophobia in the Media Since September 11th', paper presented at the University of Westminster School of Law, London, 29 September 2001, p. 3.

5 See Peter Oborne's analysis of *The Sun*'s front-page story of 7 October 2006, in which a headline, 'Muslim Hate Mob', introduced a story reporting on a group of Muslim vandals. However, it was later shown that there was no Muslim involvement in the vandalism. Oborne, Peter, 'The Shameful Islamophobia at the Heart of Britain's Press', *The Independent*, 7 July 2008.

6 '"British Troops Burn in Hell": Muslim extremists face EDL supporters in ugly scenes outside poppy-burning trial', *The Daily Mail*, 24 February 2011, and Carlin, Tom, 'Ban "Evil" Xmas, Says Cleric', *People*, 23 December 2007; Aslan, Alice, *Islamophobia in Australia*, Agora Press, Sydney, 2009, p. 46; and 'Majority Say Congressional Hearings on Alleged Extremism in American Muslim Community "Good Idea"', *Public Religion Research Institute*, 16 February 2011.

7 Brooker, Charlie, 'The News Coverage of the Norway Mass-killings was Fact-free Conjecture', *The Guardian*, 24 July 2011.

8 Mala, Elisa and Goodman, J. David, 'At Least 80 Dead in Norway Shooting', *The New York Times*, 22 July 2011.

9   Rowe, Dorothy, 'Religion: why do people believe in God?', *The Telegraph*, 30 September 2008.

10 Gordon Mathews uses the term 'cultural supermarket' in his book *Global Culture / Individual Identity: searching for home in the cultural supermarket*, Routledge, New York, 2000.

11 'About the Christian Union', *Sandown Christian Union*, www.sandowncu.co.uk/#/about/4554274288.

12 Malik, Kenan, 'A Veiled Debate', *Bergens Tidende*, 20 October 2006.

13 Wolf, Naomi, 'Behind the Veil Lives a Thriving Muslim Sexuality', *The Sydney Morning Herald*, 30 August 2008.

14 Younge, Gary, *Who Are We — and Should It Matter in the 21st Century?*, Viking, London, 2010, p. 101.

15 Ahmed, Qanta, 'The Search for Muslim Identity', *The Guardian*, 11 December 2010.

16 Younge, *Who Are We — and Should It Matter in the 21st Century?*, p. 147.

Chapter 5: God Is Love

1   Quoted in 'The Science of Love', *Your Amazing Brain*, www.youramazingbrain.org/lovesex/sciencelove.htm.

2   Carey, Benedict, 'The Brain in Love', *Los Angeles Times*, 16 December 2002.

3   Kirkpatrick, L.A. and Shaver, P.R., 'An Attachment-Theoretical Approach to Romantic Love and Religious Belief', *Personality and Social Psychology Bulletin*, vol. 18, issue 3, 1992, pp. 266–75.

4   Dennett, Daniel, *Breaking the Spell: religion as a natural phenomenon*, Viking, New York, 2006, p. 250.

5   The phrase 'powerful evolutionary benefits' appears in the blurb for Bering, Jesse, *The God Instinct: the psychology of souls, destiny, and the meaning of life*, Nicholas Brealey Publishing, London, 2010.

6   Voltaire, Anatole, 'Letter to the Author of *The Three Impostors*', 1770.

7   Harris, Sam, *Letter to a Christian Nation*, Bantam Press, London, 2007, p. 26.

8   Friedrich Nietzsche quoted in Soble, Alan (ed.), *Sex from Plato to Paglia: a philosophical encyclopedia*, vol. 2, Greenwood Press, Connecticut, 2006, p. 712.

9   James, Craig A., *The Religion Virus: why we believe in God: an evolutionist explains religion's incredible hold on humanity*, O-Books, Alresford, 2010, p. 88.

10 Warren, Ibq, 'Virgins? What Virgins?', *The Guardian*, 12 January 2002.

11 Al-Suyuti quoted in ibid.

12 Wendy Nelson's unpublished paper, 'Sexuality in Judaism' (2009), examines Jewish views on sex; text at www.mesacc. edu/~tomshoemaker/StudentPapers/JewishSexuality.html. Cults such as Ordo Templi Orientis use the technique of eroto-comatose lucidity to communicate with God.

13 Andrew Copson quoted in Peck, Tom, 'Sex Before Marriage is a Path to Misery, Teenagers Are Told', *The Independent*, 8 November 2010.

14 Laurance, Jeremy, 'Masturbation Can Be Good for the Over-50s', *The Independent*, 27 January 2009.

15 Pope Paul VI, 'Persona Humana — Declaration on Certain Questions Concerning Sexual Ethics', *Sacred Congregation of the Doctrine of the Faith*, 1975.

16 Data taken from UNAIDS, 'UNAIDS Report on the Global AIDS Epidemic', 2010.

17 Gold, Tanya, 'Ignore the Bells and the Smells and the Lovely Raphaels, the Pope's Visit to Britain is Nothing to Celebrate', *The Guardian*, 29 September 2009.

18 Pope Benedict XVI's comments quoted in Thavis, John, 'Vatican: Pope's words on condoms do not mark change in Church teaching', *Catholic Herald*, 22 December 2010.

19 Einiger, Josh, 'Hate Crime Investigation', *ABC7*, October 2009; footage at http://abclocal.go.com/wabc/video?id=7064503.

20 Leviticus 19:28 in the English Standard Version of the Bible.

21 Leviticus 20:13 in the New American Bible.

22 Masterton, Teresa, 'Man, 70, Stoned to Death For Being Gay: police', *NBC Philadelphia*, 28 March 2011.

23 See 'Homosexuality in Pakistan', *International Humanist and Ethical Union*, 4 February 2008.

24 Pumza Fihlani reported on homophobic violence and calls to 'flush out gays' in 'Religion, Politics and Africa's Homophobia', *BBC News*, 23 February 2010.

25 *The New York Times* noted that 'a leading Vatican official called homosexuality "a deviation, an irregularity, a wound"' in 'Pope Benedict Criticizes Homosexual Behavior', 22 December 2008, and *The Telegraph*'s Nick Squires reported on Pope Benedict's comments, made to a crowd at the shrine of Fatima in Portugal, in 'Pope Says Gay Marriage Is "Insidious and Dangerous"', 13 May 2010.

Chapter 6: My Father's Son
1   Shermer, Michael, 'Who Believes in God — and Why?', *Beliefnet*, 2006.
2   Harris, Sam, *The End of Faith: religion, terror, and the future of reason*, W. W. Norton, New York, 2004, p. 65.
3   ibid., p. 74.
4   Quoted in Gledhill, Ruth, 'Why Do We Believe in God? £2m study prays for answer', *Times Online*, 19 February 2008.
5   Dennett, Daniel, *Breaking the Spell: religion as a natural phenomenon*, p. 227.
6   See Diamond, Stephen, 'Radical Embitterment: the unconscious psychology of terrorists', *Psychology Today*, 26 and 29 December 2009.
7   Brink, Suzanne and Gibson, Nicholas, 'Losing Faith Without Losing Face: revising the definition of deconversion and investigating the relationship between secret disaffiliation and health', University of Cambridge, England, 2011, p. 14 and p. 23.

Chapter 7: Let There Be Light
1   For more about the New Atheism movement, see James Woods' persuasive article 'The New Atheism', *The Guardian*, 26 August 2011.
2   Read more about Camp Homeward Bound at their website: www.coalitionforthehomeless.org/programs/camp-homeward-bound.
3   Laura Silvius, a student at women's liberal arts college Bryn Mawr, wrote this paper for her Biology 103 subject in 2002. 'Religion vs Science', *Serendip*; text at http://serendip.brynmawr.edu/exchange/node/1747.
4   Statement by Professor Francisco J. Ayala given at the Templeton Prize Conference, 25 March 2010.

5   Gould, Stephen J., 'Nonoverlapping Magisteria', *Natural History*, vol. 106, March 1997, pp. 16–22.

6   Dawkins, Richard, 'When Religion Steps on Science's Turf: the alleged separation between the two is not so tidy', *Free Enquiry*, vol. 18, no. 2, Spring 1998; text at www.secularhumanism.org/library/fi/dawkins_18_2.html.

7   Mehta, Hemant, 'To Be or Not to Be ... a Dick', *Friendly Atheist*, 13 July 2010.

8   Dennett, Daniel, *Darwin's Dangerous Idea: evolution and the meaning of life*, Simon and Schuster, New York, 1995, p. 21.

9   Dobzhansky, Theodosius, 'Nothing in Biology Makes Sense Except in the Light of Evolution', *American Biology Teacher*, vol. 35, 1973, pp. 125–29.

10   'Definition of Intelligent Design', *Intelligent Design*, www.intelligentdesign.org/whatisid.php.

11   Peck, Tom and Taylor, Jerome, 'Scientist Imam Threatened over Darwinist Views', *The Independent*, 5 March 2011.

12   Quoted in Kirby, Paula, 'Crackers for Jesus', *New Statesman*, 4 September 2008.

13   John 20:29 in the New International Version of the Bible.

14   Buckman, *Can We Be Good Without God*, p. 22.

Chapter 8: Kafir

1   Crabtree, Steve and Pelham, Brett, 'What Alabamians and Iranians Have in Common', *Gallup*, 9 February 2009.

2   Mulderig, John, 'The Invention of Lying', *Catholic News Service*, 2009.

3   Gervais's comments about *The Invention of Lying* in Hiscock, John, 'Ricky Gervais Interview for *The Invention of Lying*', *The Telegraph*, 25 September 2009. His article 'Why I'm an Atheist' appeared in *The Wall Street Journal*, 19 December 2010.

4   Benson, Ophelia and Stangroom, Jeremy, *Why Truth Matters*, Continuum, New York, 2007, p. 162.

5   Russell, Bertrand, *Why I Am Not a Christian: and other essays on religion and related subjects*, Routledge, London, 2010, p. 10.

6   Armstrong, Karen, *The Case for God*, Vintage, London, 2010, p. 8.

7   ibid., p. 29 and p. 19.
8   'US Religious Knowledge Survey', *The Pew Forum on Religion and Public Life*, 28 September 2010.
9   Landsberg, Mitchell, 'Atheists, Agnostics Most Knowledgeable About Religion, Survey Says', *Los Angeles Times*, 28 September 2010.
10 Armstrong, *A History of God*, p. 37.
11 Benson and Stangroom, *Why Truth Matters*, p. 179.
12 'Rebecca Newberger on *36 Arguments for the Existence of God*', *Amazon*, 2010.
13 Warraq, Ibn, *Why I Am Not a Muslim*, Prometheus Books, New York, 2003, p. xv.

Epilogue

1   White, T.H., *The Once and Future King*, HarperCollins, London, 2001 (first published 1958), p. 193–94.

ACKNOWLEDGEMENTS

This book began with a conversation at my school gate. I was saying goodbye to Anthony Grayling after I had spent the morning interviewing him for my film, *Why is Science Important?* Just before he left, he turned to me and said, 'You know, you should write a book.' A few months later, I emailed Anthony to ask if he had meant what he said, and if so, whether he might help me. He invited me out for a cup of tea, told me how to write a book proposal, and assured me that he'd do everything he could to ensure the publication of any book I wrote. Anthony has been true to his word, and my words are inadequate to express the gratitude I feel towards this wonderful man.

Anthony introduced me to Catherine Clarke, who, also over a cup of tea, agreed that I should write a book … but not the one that I had proposed to her. Instead, she guided me towards the book I eventually wrote, and worked tirelessly to secure me a book deal. Again, I can't thank Catherine enough for her belief in the book and in me.

I hope that Henry Rosenbloom already knows how grateful I am to him for committing to publishing this book, but I also owe him thanks for introducing me to Julia Carlomagno, my editor at Scribe. Julia told me that I could write whatever I wanted in these acknowledgements, which is a pity, as I'm sure they would be far more eloquent if she had cast her eyes over them before letting them go to print. She has made this book a far better one than I ever could have written on my own, and she has done that without ever causing me any stress or heartache. It has been a joy working with her. Any remaining mistakes and flaws in the book are entirely mine.

I would also like to express my thanks to Iain Dale and Sam Carter at Biteback for publishing the book in the UK, and to Namkwan Cho for his jacket design.

But Julia has not been my only editor, and I must thank Lizzie Ashe for her wisdom, guidance, and, above all, support, from the moment I started writing this book. I'm also grateful to David Shariatmadari, Alok Jha, and Mark Henderson for giving me opportunities to write for their publications, and to try out some of my thinking on their readers.

Rubel Ahmed, Nazmul Hussain, and Pasha Kamal deserve a special thank-you for kindly losing many games of poker so that I could work on this book without experiencing financial hardship, and for continuing to be loving, supportive friends, despite the fact that I am a bacon-eating kafir.

Soon after I started secondary school, Jonathan Hassid took me to his house and introduced me to his mother, Jane.

I'm grateful to Jonny for that, even more than I am for the Michael Jackson tickets.

I often called Jonathan Sanderson when I was struggling with a particular idea or passage in the book. He had a brilliant knack for listening to me and repeating back what I'd said, so that I would hang up the phone with renewed confidence in what I was trying to write.

Sam Thenabadu married my sister while I was writing this book, but he was a member of our family long before then. His enthusiasm for the book surpasses my own, and I hope it lives up to his expectations.

Ben Payne has been my friend and role model since I was 11, and I'm grateful to his parents for giving me another brother and for letting us experience 'proper' Christmas dinners at their home.

Kylie Sturgess and Warren Bonett were instrumental in helping me get a book deal, supporting me all the way from Australia despite never having met me in person. They exemplify the kindness of strangers who become friends over the internet.

David Pearson and Miriam Rosenbloom did a wonderful job in designing the cover, and my thanks also to Ian See for proofreading the text.

I have chewed the ears off countless people in talking about this book, but those conversations were often instrumental in shaping my thoughts. I'd like to thank the following people for allowing me to pick their brains: Luke Donnellan, Jon Stubbings, Colin Watts, Lorne Stefanini, Ellie Clay, Susan

Green, Marcus Chown, Kenan Malik, Ian Simmons, Elin Roberts, Ben Craven, Adam Rutherford, Tom Whyntie, Crispian Jago, Jacquelynn Potter, Nathalia Chubin-Norman, Jessie Stewart, Suzanne Brink, Ruth Seeley, Anna Starkey, Stephen Curry, Ronan McDonald, Lynda Charlesworth, Katherine Coyne, David Waldock, Ginger Lawrence, Mike McRae, Ritch Steele, Anwar Khan, and, of course, my students. Apologies to anyone I've missed, but I'll buy you a drink the next time I see you.

I have been grateful to Bruce Grimmett and Phil Cook ever since I was at primary school, not only for being great teachers, but also for doing so much to get me off to a good start in life. This book is as much their doing as it is mine.

Also published by Biteback

THE MYTH OF CHOICE
PERSONAL RESPONSIBILITY IN A WORLD OF LIMITS

KENT GREENFIELD

We are all fixated on the idea of choice. As people we love to feel that we have choice, and little offends us more than when that notion is taken away from us. Western political theory is based on the consent of the governed. Our legal systems are built upon the argument that people freely bear responsibility for the choices they make. At the heart of consumer culture is the idea that we can have it our way. But what if choice is more limited than we like to think?

In *The Myth of Choice*, Kent Greenfield uses scores of real-life stories to explore the modern fixation on choice and our confused responses to it, but also offers useful suggestions to help us become better decision-makers as individuals.

256pp paperback, £12.99

Available from all good bookshops
www.bitebackpublishing.com